Leaving ADDIE for SAM

An Agile Model for Developing the Best Learning Experiences

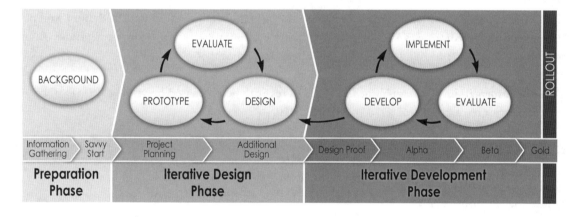

Michael Allen

with Richard Sites

ASTD Press is an internationally renowned source of insightful and practical information on workplace learning and performance topics, including training basics, evaluation and return-on-investment, instructional systems development, e-learning, leadership, and career development.

Ordering information: Books published by ASTD Press can be purchased by visiting ASTD's website at store.astd.org or by calling 800.628.2783 or 703.683.8100.

Library of Congress Control Number: 2009940017

ISBN-10: 1-56286-711-3
ISBN-13: 978-1-56286-711-9

ASTD Press Editorial Staff:
Director: Glenn Saltzman
Community of Practice Manager, Learning & Development: Juana Llorens
Senior Associate Editor: Ashley McDonald
Design and Production: Brendan Stern
Cover Design: Lon Levy

Printed by Versa Press, Inc., East Peoria, IL, www.versapress.com

Contents

Preface vii
Dedication xii
Acknowledgments xiii

Part I: A New Model for Instructional Product Design and Development 1

Chapter 1: Traditional Design Models Disappoint 3
We Need Better Learning 4
Causes of Poor Learning Programs 5

Chapter 2: Instructional Systems Design 11
Instructional Design 11
Familiarity Begets Credibility 13
Process Selection 14
What Was ADDIE Originally? 14
Learning to Adapt 17
The Best Model 17

Chapter 3: Anatomy of Effective Learning Events 21
E-Learning Brings Issues to Light 21
Fundamental Characteristics 22
Fundamental Components of Interactive Learning Events 23

Chapter 4: Successive Approximation Model 1 29
The Ideal Process Model 29
Successive Approximation 33

Chapter 5: Successive Approximation Model 2 39
Preparation Phase 40
Iterative Design Phase 42
Iterative Development Phase 45

Chapter 6: Are You the One? 49
Setting and Maintaining Expectations 50
Dynamically Adjusting Design and Project Variables 51
Keeping the Focus on Behavior Change 51
Being a Learner Advocate 52
Are You a SAM Leader? 52

Part II: Using the Successive Approximation Model 55

Chapter 7: Preparation Phase 57
Backgrounding 58
The Savvy Start 60
Planning the Savvy Start 62
Building a Savvy Start Team 62
The Savvy Start Agenda 65
Customizing the Savvy Start 69
Preparing the Room 70
Conducting the Savvy Start 70
Prototyping and Evaluation 80
Wrap Up 81

Chapter 8: Protyping 83
Sketching 83
Why Build Prototypes 84
e-Sketches 87
The Essence of a Prototype 92
e-Learning Prototypes 94
Three Prototypes, Plus or Minus One 98

Chapter 9: Constructing the Prototype 99
The Helpful Prototyper 99
Prototyping Tools 100
Starting to Build Your Prototype 104
Review the Prototype 105
Wrap Up 108

Chapter 10: Setting the Target 109
Goals 109
Instructional Objectives 110
Pre-Existing Content 115
Assessment 117
Summary 119

Chapter 11: Designing for Success 121
Breadth Versus Depth 121
Look Ahead 122

Chapter 12: Project Planning 127
Initial Planning 128
Pragmatic Considerations 131
Sample Project Plan 134

Chapter 13: Additional Design 157
Completing the Design 157

Part III: Iterative Development Phase 159

Chapter 14: Creating the Design Proof 161
Avoiding the Best Idea 162
The Design Proof 162
Writing Course Content 164

Chapter 15: Iterative Evaluation 169
Managing Reviews 172
Setting Expectations for Iterative Reviews 176
Conducting a Learner Review 178
Quality Assurance in SAM 179
Evaluating the Course 179

Chapter 16: Getting to Gold 181
The Deliverables 181
Let the Good Times Roll 187
Debrief 187

References 190
Other Selected Works by Michael Allen 192
About the Authors 193
Index 197

PREFACE

Leave ADDIE, you say? And why would I do that?

If this is your question, I'm quite inclined to say you should stick with ADDIE. I'm very supportive of any process that reliably and efficiently produces desired results. If ADDIE does this for you, then you're a fortunate person. You have your tool, your comfort zone, your success, and I do sincerely congratulate you.

I mean it.

I used to use and teach the ADDIE process, or what I considered something of *the standard* ADDIE process. I taught it with assurance and conviction. The ADDIE process of analysis, design, development, implementation, and evaluation is logical, thoughtful, and comprehensive. There's little in the process one can argue with in terms of relevance and importance.

Did it work?

Well, yes and no. As I'll describe in a moment, I witnessed its use in a variety of settings over a great many projects. It produced products, yes. It gave managers an understandable process that appeared quite manageable. It had measures of progress threaded through it, yielding status data to report. There's a lot to like about it from a managerial point of view. It's definitely left-brained—comforting to the concrete thinker.

But did it produce good learning products? Did teams feel productive? Were they proud of their work? I have to say no, not so often in what I've seen.

◆　◆　◆

My career in instructional product development began with a PhD in educational psychology. I had the uncanny good fortune of meandering through rare opportunities to learn from putting instructional theories and knowledge about human learning to work. Even in my graduate program, I had a unique opportunity to work with a newly built National Science Foundation center designed to demonstrate and validate the latest in instructional approaches and technology. Working with the center I had a chance to experiment and ultimately develop the means to guide learners individually, to help them discover their personal learning styles, to continually measure and fortify their growing confidence, and to prepare them for success.

I also received grant support from the psychology department to investigate uses of technology to help unwieldy numbers of freshman psychology students work at an individualized pace toward mastery of the subject. Then, with support from IBM, I developed software to analyze student progress and validate which instructional paradigms were most effective with particular learning styles and to measure assessment validity. After I was graduated from the PhD program, the university put me in a rare and wonderful position—teaching faculty members the means of offering better learning experiences to their students.

Later, with an offer no one could refuse, I went to work with Control Data's PLATO project to develop computer-assisted learning for Control Data Institute enrollees. As Control Data's work with PLATO grew and our staff expanded from a couple dozen to hundreds, everyone's work became more specialized. Becoming director of research and development, a position I held for a decade, I focused primarily on two areas: research on human learning and tools for curriculum development/management. A group separate from mine was formed solely for courseware production.

In my current company, formed after developing Authorware, taking it to market, and combining with Macromind/Paracomp to form Macromedia, we have built custom learning solution studios on both U.S. coasts and in the Midwest. For more than 18 years we have produced huge volumes of instructional products, including instructor-led courses, e-learning, and blended programs. The work of our studios has our lobby proudly overflowing with awards and superlative commendations.

◆ ◆ ◆

The point of this embarrassing reminiscence? I've had an opportunity to design, build, manage, and observe the production of an extraordinary number of instructional products: education and training, large budget and small, complex and simple, technology and no technology, successful and not. My hope in setting fingers to keyboard and mouse here is to channel greater success from the tremendous effort that goes into each and every instructional product.

At Control Data, where a huge courseware production organization was built, a cornerstone project was undertaken. It was the development of a curriculum to teach effective courseware design and development—essentially the ADDIE of analysis, design, development, implementation, and evaluation. While I'd like to digress into a discussion of the irony of how this ill-fated undertaking struggled painfully to launch an instructionally viable and useful product, I will state only that after missing deadline after deadline, repeatedly exceeding budget, and producing power struggles with career-threatening tensions, it started my questioning of ADDIE. As far as I can recall, very few—if any—of the participants in this project were proud of the product produced and wished to claim credit for it. If even the ADDIE experts couldn't use ADDIE to teach ADDIE, something was amiss.

As with the majority of ADDIE projects, a product did emerge. ADDIE is pretty good at assuring something will emerge. The product went through at least several major revisions after its introduction, so I don't believe it is unfair to assess the project as more of a valiant effort than a stunning success. This shouldn't have been the case, and I hope, dear reader, it won't be yours.

Good instruction is inspirational. It captures both the power of knowledge and skill as well as the joy of becoming competent. Good learning experiences aren't just about facts, they are about becoming a more proficient, capable, and valuable person. To my taste, ADDIE—a process that comprises many valuable tasks—fails to recognize the necessary creativeness and inventiveness of the work, to allow for and support exploration and changing ideas that need to arise within and as part of the process.

A good and wise friend advised me many years ago when I was designing and building an authoring system for PLATO: "It's too early to build a tool until you've defined the process it is intended to support," he said. This fine advice led me to seriously question ADDIE, especially in the wake of the products I saw it producing and the tension people felt using it. This questioning ultimately led me to advice of my own. *It's too early to define a process unless you've defined the product you want it to produce.* The starting place is to decide what we want in our instructional products.

Meaningful, memorable, and motivational. Many readers will know I had to say it sooner or later, as these are the characteristics I feel are imperative for the success of instructional events. Lacking any of these three, an instructional experience fails to be what it should and needs to be. Today, this seems like a certainty to me (although I strongly endorsed ADDIE years ago, too, so we need to be careful). But, yes, I shout it out at every chance. Meaningful, memorable, motivational. The big three Ms.

Knowing that the destination is the big three Ms, we can tailor a process that pushes in the right direction. It's in the pursuit of just such a process that Successive Approximation was born.

◆　◆　◆

This is not a book about instructional design—at least it wasn't intended to be. Because product and process are so closely interdependent, it was impossible to write all that needed to be shared without overlapping into topics of instructional design more than once. I admit that I wrote and removed many segments in which I couldn't avoid delving into instructional design. I had to write them for my own satisfaction. But then as they seemed too preachy and muddying, I pulled them. Indeed, I've written about instructional design to the best of my ability many other places, and for those interested in my opinions, they aren't hard to find.

But even with such attempts at considerate weeding, it's not all gone. I can't help but remind us all, over and over again, that instruction isn't primarily about presenting information. And learning isn't primarily about knowing things. The goal is always about performance. *What can people do with their new knowledge? What skills are necessary for success?* One never succeeds without doing something. Deciding not to do something is, of course, making the decision not to—and thus *is* doing something, the something one might have learned was appropriate. Follow? Even in academia, we want our students to be good problem solvers and good conversationalists. We want them to realize when the knowledge they have is applicable, and we want them to apply it successfully. It's about doing things.

So I hope you will tolerate my occasional lapses into topics of instructional design. I believe they are relevant to understanding why characteristics of the successive approximation model (SAM) are important. I hope also that you will forgive my tendency to focus on e-learning. e-Learning products tend to fly solo—to stand more on their own unaided by a sympathetic and charismatic instructor who can fill in the gaps, provide instant explanations and remediation, and motivate those who need to keep focused and energized. If the product doesn't do it, it won't get done.

e-Learning therefore requires the most care in design and construction. Perhaps it's the best test of whether a process can produce desired products. But please don't read, through the fault of my biased attention to e-learning, that successive approximation is appropriate only for e-learning or is itself biased toward it. Indeed, successive approximation is, in my experience, a far superlative process for the production of any instructional product. I hope very much that you will find it so yourself.

For Nancy Olson

With whom we at Allen Interactions have had the pleasure of partnering for many years. Nancy's leadership at ASTD has enlightened and inspired many of us in the learning industry by tirelessly creating opportunities for us to share and learn from each other. She paved the way for this publication to become a reality through her advocacy of our unique and effective e-learning design and development approach and has delighted in seeing the enthusiastic reactions to it. Nancy was instrumental in creating the prestigious ASTD e-Learning Instructional Design Certificate Programs through which we have shared SAM, CCAF, and other methods of achieving "meaningful, memorable, and motivational" learning. Nancy has, and continues to be, a true partner and confidante, continually dazzling us with her communication skills, insights, friendship, and trust.

Nancy, this book is for you.

Acknowledgments

This book is the product of experience and wisdom shared so willingly with me over many years. I appreciate the opportunities so many clients have given us to refine the successive approximation model I started exploring way back with the PLATO project at Control Data Corporation, beginning in the mid-1970s. I would like to thank Wiley and Pfeiffer for allowing me to refer back to and include some material from my e-Learning Library Series.

In constructing this book, I'm particularly indebted to Richard Sites, who co-wrote many sections with me. Marty Lipshutz, my long-term business partner and friend helped with the example project plan and handled extra business responsibilities so I could have time to write. Ethan Edwards, our chief instructional designer, provided some very helpful examples of prototypes. Nicole Mellas, Linda Rening, and Lisa Stortz provided so many good ideas, corrected my oversights, and caught errors. They, and our custom e-learning studios, helped keep recommendations firmly grounded in realities. And, with the world's most extraordinary patience, Amy Pahl stayed with me through the process of getting ideas down, organized, and published.

PART 1

A New Model for Instructional Product Design and Development

This book defines and shares a process for efficient and flexible design and development of engaging and effective learning products. While the principles of instructional design and the characteristics of successful instructional events are discussed, the intent of this book is to provide a foundation for teams to work with an iterative process to build wonderful learning experiences. At the very least, I hope the book provides a basis for taking the risk of trying something different to achieve something spectacular.

Part I focuses on problems with instructional systems development (ISD) models such as ADDIE that have become traditional and yet are variously defined and, at least in many instances, less successful in producing quality products and managing constraints than they might be. We then turn to an alternative, the Successive Approximation Model (SAM), which, with similarities to such contemporary software development models as Agile, Extreme Programming (XP), and SCRUM, uses iteration, short work cycles, and other techniques to produce the best possible product regardless of situational constraints.

CHAPTER 1

Traditional Design Models Disappoint

The traditional processes used to create learning too often churn out rather disappointing programs. The regrettable impact has been felt throughout organizations, by the training department to the learners and on to management and shareholders. Training departments take too long and spend too much money creating training programs that are either late, have little impact, or both. Learners waste precious time and energy with low-quality training products, even dropping out when they can. Management allocates constraining budgets that permit little to no return-on-investment. Shareholders find competing organizations have not missed opportunities to outperform theirs and wonder why.

Anyone developing instructional programs faces numerous challenges. To ensure the most success in design and development efforts, developers need a model that recognizes these challenges and provides a clear path to success.

Successful models work within existing constraints. They
- investigate alternatives
- deliver projects on time
- deliver projects within budget
- use available delivery resources
- use labor-saving tools
- keep stakeholders informed (if not involved).

Successful models achieve valued results. They
- develop learner skills
- improve performance (change behavior)
- deliver manageable programs
- provide a sustained return-on-investment.

WE NEED BETTER LEARNING

Instruction provided by companies and organizations today is often overburdened with content and lots of text. And it's much too light on learning experiences and opportunities to practice. Even e-learning technology that stands ready to present interactive video, animation, and graphics, tends to be laden with text-heavy presentations delivered in a page-turning format. This type of learning is tiresome and boring. And sadly, that's not the worst part.

Boring instruction is costly, damaging, ineffective, and wasteful. Consider the following effects that boring instruction has on learners.

Inattention: Gaining learner attention is critical to enabling instruction. No attention means no learning. Boring instruction dampens the learner's desire to learn, ability to focus, and willingness to practice as needed to develop new skills and performance behaviors.

Negative attitudes: Even after spending all the time and money necessary to create an instructional program, if it provides learners a boring experience, it will likely result in both a lack of learning and a dislike of the method of instruction. Many have learned to dislike classroom instruction, while others have learned to dislike e-learning or social learning events, all because of boring experiences with them.

Subject aversion: A bad experience carries an even greater likelihood that learners will come to dislike the material being presented. Deterring learners from acquiring critical skills and knowledge can result in failures that, in turn, seriously hinder possibilities of future learning. Learners can develop a hindering self-image, such as *I'm no good at public speaking/math/sales,* which may persist through the remainder of their lives.

Learner disrespect: Learners are annoyed and even insulted by the organization that is ready to waste their time, presumably just to save instructional development costs. Learners do make the deduction. *They really didn't put anything into this, and yet they require us all to agonize through it. What a waste! I've got work to do.* Learners typically look for easy paths, but when the pain is extreme they find means to escape. *This course is so bad, I'll have to pay someone to take it for me.* This happens—and not infrequently.

With organizations constantly challenged to demonstrate that employees are individually valued and that their time and contributions are important, requiring learners to endure boring programs is a surefire way of fostering antipathy, if not animosity and attrition. These aren't usually the goals of an instructional program.

Since we all know intuitively that boring instruction is bad and that it has minimal value, the fact that there is so much of it is bewildering. Why do schools offer deathly boring courses and companies offer boring training—sometimes with exuberance and fanfare?

CAUSES OF POOR LEARNING PROGRAMS

There are many reasons why organizations settle for boring and ineffective learning programs. A few that come to mind are that organizations:
- fail to manage project risks effectively
- spend too much of a project's resources and energy on upfront analysis
- spend too little time and energy exploring alternative design options
- focus on content presentation, accuracy, and comprehensiveness (instead of the learning experience)
- fail to involve sponsors, stakeholders, and learners throughout the design process
- yield to design by committee and the opinions of organizationally dominant individuals
- employ outdated methods.

Managing Risks

Traditional training design methods are quite linear, segmented processes that require the completion and approval of work done at each phase before moving forward to the next. Managers must review and approve design and specification documents, for example, before development can commence. These methods seek to limit risks the team faces at each subsequent phase of the process. Approval at the conclusion of each phase releases the team, it is hoped, from any liability should the final product not provide the expected results or meet learners' needs.

The requirement within these traditional processes to gain explicit approval drives training departments to create designs that are readily communicated through specification documents or storyboards, both of which are notorious for multiple interpretations, no matter how detailed they may be. Designers often go to extreme lengths to avoid ambiguity, yet both subsequent developers and approvers frequently envision different final products. Consequences of presenting stakeholders with a final product that is not exactly what they thought they approved can include considerable discord and disruption. Therefore, if a learning event is hard to describe, teams will set the idea aside rather than risk disapproval and failure. Learning experiences with the greatest potential are particularly susceptible to being discarded because they can be difficult to describe clearly, require exploration before they can be evaluated, and are likely to result in extended discussion—all costly risks.

Analysis Paralysis

Design documentation typically begins with the justification of why instruction is being developed. Early in traditional processes, the focus is on complete and accurate analysis of the need and alternative solutions. Regardless of the time and money spent, however, this analysis is often incomplete and inaccurate—almost by necessity, because so much "non-productive" time can be spent on it, relevant data are hard to acquire, available information is often misleading, and situations change while the analysis is underway. For example, the analysis may be based on ineffective learning programs currently in place. Erroneous and misleading conclusions such as "e-learning doesn't work for soft skills" can easily be reached when the real problem was with course design rather than delivery medium. Deep analysis is difficult, expensive, and time consuming. When analysis takes a big chunk out of available resources, the resulting learning program may have to be reduced to something very basic and perhaps quite unengaging.

Nothing but the Facts

Many people have grown up with and succeeded in spite of "tell-and-test" instruction—the typical approach of exposing learners to a body of information and then testing for retention. They have listened to years of instructor presentations, read shelves of books and articles, watched hours of videos (or filmstrips), done countless hours of homework, and taken who knows how many quizzes and tests. The pattern is simple. Information is supplied over a period of time preceding a quiz or test constructed of multiple-choice questions. Repeat.

The process is nicely manageable. Everyone starts on the same day, finishes on the same day. Grades indicate varying outcomes. And there will be varying outcomes, of course, because not everyone can learn the same amount in the same time. Instructors present an amount of content that can be learned by most. For some learners, it's not enough; for others, it's too much.

This is probably not the time or place to assail this "tried-and-true" method, but the obvious variance in results it achieves should raise questions. Does it matter whether a portion of learners fail? Does it matter whether learners can actually do anything better or differently? Does it matter whether learners were productive with their time and are eager to perform? Does it matter that some learners wasted their time because they only needed a small part of the content, if any?

Although it can be harder than one might think to agree on what content to present or even what the "facts" are, a basic pattern of presenting information followed by testing for comprehension or retention is an easy design for approvers to understand. Preparation of the content is as straightforward as it can be. Agreement and approvals can be won in short order. Off we go. Yet you may find learners and instructors thinking, *I wish our courses weren't so boring.*

Too Many Facts

To reach consensus with a tell-and-test paradigm as described above, we just have to add in all the facts that everyone feels are relevant. Focus becomes on being thorough and complete. *Exhaustive* is a better word. *Get it all in there. Legal needs to add more. Sure. Can't fight legal.*

Training designers the world over know that their two biggest problems are likely to be 1) having to deal with too much content—each and every piece of which has a staunch advocate, and 2) getting timely approvals throughout the process. Nobody wants to sign off on the work until it's done. When it's done, people want to make changes. The most likely change: Add more content.

What Learners Want and Need

I've come to expect it now, but most organizations are certain they know what interests and doesn't interest their learners. They "know" what their learners know and don't know. They "know" what learners can and can't do. They "know" what their learners like and dislike, how they'll respond, and what they'll do. They know. *We don't need to waste time involving learners. Besides, they don't know what they don't know. We know.*

They are so certain they know learner needs and preferences that they adamantly refuse to involve learners in the process of designing learning solutions. The problem is that they are rarely—very rarely—correct.

An Anecdote

When working toward my teaching certificate in college, my advisor and I had read of a technique that involved learners even in selecting course topics. It seemed extreme to ask students what they should study, but we decided I should try it anyway.

On the first day of the high school psychology class I was teaching, I asked students to move their seats to the side and sit with me on the floor. I said, "OK, this is Psych 101. What should we study?" The theory was that with only a little guidance, learners would zero in on what's relevant to them and come close to indicating what they needed to know without actually knowing what they didn't know.

Did it work? Amazingly, yes! There was much conversation that gave me tremendous insight into what these young adults found interesting. It helped me understand their impressions of psychology—right and wrong—and what they wanted to learn about people and behavior.

We discussed various types of psychological research, from abnormal behavior (of course) to experimental, social, clinical, and so on. They set their priorities, and I had no trouble determining how I was going to work fundamental concepts into the outline they constructed. They learned a surprising amount about psychology in this discussion, and I learned an amazing amount of extremely important information about them.

It's a huge mistake not to involve learners in the design of learning programs. Huge.

Anyone Can Do This

Instructional design is a profession. Not everyone gets the important fact that designing good instruction requires considerable knowledge, skill, and practice. A frequent cause of poor learning programs is that individuals are involved who, recalling their many experiences as a student, have strong opinions about what makes good instruction. Simply having been a student makes them no more of an instructional designer than having had their teeth cared for makes them a dentist.

For project leaders to be advocates of professional design, it helps very much to have examples of both poor and excellent instructional programs. Contrasts between the two can convince project leaders more readily than simply showing excellence. Demonstrating these programs can quell dominant personalities who think that anyone can design training—that putting together a presentation and a document filled with content will cause learners to change their performance—and encourage others to speak up in favor of competent approaches.

It also helps to be something of a psychologist—to be able to draw out opinions from those who just agree to avoid tension and quiet those who insist on voicing their every opinion. Regardless of the leader's talents and team composition, it helps to have a process that can make alternatives evident and equalize opinions so the goal of just coming to an agreement doesn't substitute for the goal of creating effective learning experiences.

We Have Our Process

While every project has risks to manage, information to gather, a tendency to present information—too much information—with minimal context, opinionated persons to manage, and a readiness to assume what learners know, need, and want, organizations also tend to believe in and hold tightly to the process they are using. Departures from a familiar process can intimidate and frighten even the most adventurous and those who seem ready to try something different. But many organizations are using outdated methods that, on close inspection, may actually exacerbate common project problems rather than resolve them.

Threatening and disorienting as change can be, it seems there are many reasons to aspire to something better.

CHAPTER 2

Instructional Systems Design

Never before have so many people been tasked with creating instructional activities, materials, and programs for learners in schools, businesses, and organizations. Many have little formal training in instructional design, if any (Carliner and Driscoll, 2009). They are guided by their intuition, their observations of what they have seen others do, and their experiences as a learner. Of those who have received instruction on instructional design, an instructional systems design (ISD) model most likely guides their work. ISD models frequently divide the process into phases, such as analysis, design, development, implementation, and evaluation. It is from this logical, commonsense series of phases that the "ADDIE" name is derived.

INSTRUCTIONAL DESIGN

What is it? The definition of instructional design "can revolve around numerous perspectives: process, discipline, science, and reality" (Crawford, 2004, p. 414). Piskurich defines instructional design as "simply a process for helping you create effective training in an efficient manner" and helping "you ask the right questions, make the right decisions, and produce a product that is as useful and useable as your situation requires and allows" (2000, p. 1).

These general and perhaps indeterminate definitions reflect the fact that instructional design is basically multidimensional decision making. It's a process historically viewed much like that of a building architect. The expected outcome from an instructional designer is a blueprint to guide the development of learning experiences. The designer is expected to produce specifications of a product that can be developed within time and cost budgets, and the product should achieve defined goals while meeting a variety of constraints and preferences. Although the delivered blueprint needs to be very clear, understandable, and as simple as possible, the design task can be very complex due to the number of considerations. There are many questions to be answered, such as:

- Who is to be taught what and what are the learners' current capabilities?
- What types of skills are to be learned?
- What delivery platforms are available?
- Are other learning experiences needed and available?
- What are the coordination opportunities and restrictions?
- Who will do the development and what are their capabilities?
- Are representative learners available for trial runs?
- Who is available to assist with content information gathering, synthesis, and organization?
- Are media resources available and sufficient?
- Will licensed materials be needed and are they affordable?
- Is there a hard deadline for delivery of the instructional product?
- What approvals are necessary?
- Who will review and approve?
- What is the availability of people who must review and approve?
- How is learning success defined and how will it be measured?
- How is project success defined and how will it be measured?

Identifying the variables that will impact decisions and collecting accurate data are two important steps to avoid going off in wrong directions. It is the awareness of this importance that places analysis as the first step in ISD and as critical input to design. Because there are many variables that define instructional needs, many tasks to assess each of those variables, and potential problems if a variable is overlooked or inaccurately measured, ISD has become more structured and formalized over the years. As Gustafson and Branch state, it is "a system of procedures for developing educational and training programs in a consistent and reliable fashion" (2001, p. 17).

There is, indeed, comfort and security in having a defined set of steps, checklists, and criteria. Were I asked to do a totally unfamiliar job, such as replace an automobile engine, I'd really want such a system of procedures.

FAMILIARITY BEGETS CREDIBILITY

The high level view of the ADDIE model of ISD, its five sequential phases of analysis, design, development, implementation, and evaluation, makes tremendous sense as a system of procedures. It has been widely used in various adaptations. Indeed, the ADDIE acronym has become so ubiquitous in the training industry that Bichelmeyer (2005) didn't even consider defining it until the final draft of her article about its role in the industry.

In actuality however, when people refer to ADDIE, about all we know is that they divide tasks into analysis, design, development, implementation, and evaluation phases. Beyond that, one knows fairly little because of the wide variances in application. Reports and conference papers on how ADDIE has been modified and adapted are voluminous. It seems nearly all organizations find modification desirable if not mandatory, and even then, designers and developers regularly report much deviation from their own formalized adaptations, indicating *it's not what we actually do*. Iteration, in particular, is seen not as an option but a necessity; yet the basic ADDIE model is not iterative.

Faith in ADDIE has been strong, perhaps from tradition as much as any other reason, but ADDIE is far from the most up to date, effective, reliable, and proven process for building quality learning. The foundational notions of ADDIE are quite old now and address problems and opportunities that have changed dramatically and significantly over the years, and there are perhaps hundreds of thousands of developed courses that would suggest the process does not ensure many measures of quality. Widespread use, a memorable acronym, a defined process with the appeal and appearance of manageability, together with many sources of information and training on the process, are commendable attributes envied by all marketeers. Unfortunately, reliable product quality is not foremost among its credits.

Indeed, the ADDIE model is not without considerable criticism. The model has been criticized for being "too systematic, that is, too linear, too inflexible, too constraining, and even too time consuming to implement" (Kruse, 2009). Other criticisms range from the model's inability to take "advantage of digital technologies" to the model not providing an accurate representation of the "way instructional designers do their work" (Bichelmeyer, 2005, p. 4).

PROCESS SELECTION

There is more to the relationship between effective design and process than just efficiency. Processes can affect quality, creativity, and accuracy just as much as they do efficiency and timeliness. When we select a process, we are also selecting the type of product we want. For example, does the process promote experimentation with ideas and media or look to theoretical analysis for guidance? Experimentation with learner involvement early in the process can generate ideas before costly development work is undertaken. Does the process emphasize making the learning experience engaging and enduring through practice, or does the process emphasize content coverage and thoroughness? Addressing the learning experience to make it a meaningful and memorable one can determine what content does and doesn't belong, whereas emphasis on content thoroughness almost inevitably leads to boring, burdensome, and ineffective presentations for passive absorption by the learner.

When we select a process, we are also selecting the type of product we want.

Definition and sequence of tasks or events delineate a process. The five-stage ADDIE process offers a linear approach—completing one stage before moving on to the next (Crawford, 2004; Molenda, Reiguluth, and Nelson, 2003), although common adaptations loosen the linearity of the prerequisite chain in various ways. Changes make a big difference, of course, and a changed process must be renamed and considered a different process. Not having done so has led to much of the confusion about what ADDIE is and isn't. It isn't helpful to suggest a named process is anything we're doing today. Processes need a crisp definition in order to be understood, evaluated, selected, and applied.

WHAT WAS ADDIE ORIGINALLY?

To further complicate the usefulness of adapted ADDIE models, there is no clear agreement on what the base model is. Molenda states when authors proffer adaptations and narrative descriptions based on the ADDIE model they "are essentially creating and disseminating their own models as there does not appear to be an original, authoritative version of the ADDIE model to be revealed and interpreted" (2003, p. 36).

While the origins of this model are unclear, the underlying process has its origins in the U.S. armed forces (Molenda, 2003). The intent was to develop a system for the design of instruction that would be more "effective, efficient, and relevant than less rigorous approaches to planning instruction" (Gustafson and Branch, 2002). Figure 2-1 is a diagram of the early systems model that served as the predecessor to current ISD models and eventually ADDIE.

Figure 2-1. Early Version of ADDIE: Five Phases of ISD

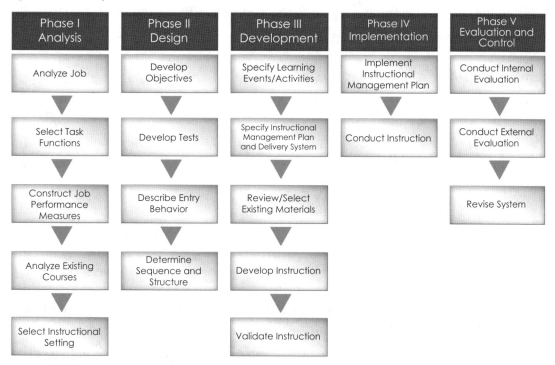

Source: 2011, Clark, D.; adapted from Branson, Rayner, Cox, Furman, King, Hannum, 1975.
Figure courtesy of Donald Clark.

Graphic representation of a model with so many major steps is quite helpful to gain a quick, overview notion. Reading through the uniform size boxes, however, one immediately recognizes that the magnitude of each step is not represented by the size of the box. That is, the varying levels of time and effort needed to complete steps are not represented. Nor is the complex relationship among the steps. Indeed, were one to connect steps that have relationships to each other, the diagram would be so encumbered with lines that it would be impossible to read.

In what we understand to be the foundational notion of ADDIE, dependency relationships are implied by the sequence. That is, specifying learning events (Step 1, Phase III) is dependent on developing objectives (Step 1, Phase II), but determining sequence and structure (Step 4, Phase II) is not dependent on reviewing existing materials (Step 3, Phase III). Practicalities, however, might suggest otherwise.

This model is classified today as a waterfall process—that is, all steps in one phase are completed in sequence before moving on to the next phase. The waterfall concept, so called because water does not flow backward or uphill, is illustrated in Figure 2-2.

Figure 2-2. ADDIE as a Waterfall Process

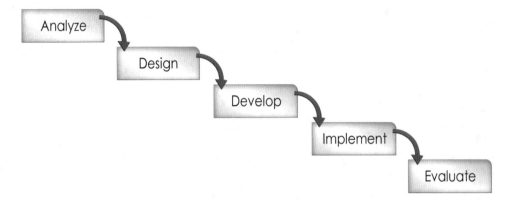

What we know today, from many years of experience, is that there is a vital experimental and exploratory exercise that needs to be undertaken in the process of instructional design. Although we have much research on human learning, brain function, perception, and communication of information to guide us, the undertaking of instructional product design is very complex. There are too many variances in each project to make success with them as simple as applying our knowledge. We need to use our knowledge to formulate our best guess, our first "approximation" of an ideal design, and then find ways to evaluate it. We need to take quicker, smaller steps so that we can receive the additional guidance of evaluation before we have spent all our project's time and resources on only one guess.

Evaluation to catch mistakes toward the end of the process, as with ADDIE, is better than not correcting them at all. But there are risks. Continuous evaluation and correction as early as possible returns valuable rewards.

Waiting to make corrections toward the end of the process invites trouble.

LEARNING TO ADAPT

In an effort to address the limitations of the linear waterfall approach of the early ADDIE models, some have proposed an ADDIE model that is iterative or cyclical. Figure 2-3 is a diagram of a modification of the ADDIE model, modified to support iteration and provide greater flexibility.

Figure 2-3. A Modification of ADDIE

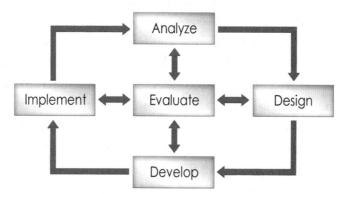

This diagram is one of many modified ADDIE models. Others differ in the arrangement of the model phases, use and placement of double-headed arrows, and so on. These modifications, while desirable in many instances, muddle the definition of ADDIE. Although any process that contains analysis, design, development, implementation, and evaluation could be called an ADDIE process, what process wouldn't involve these tasks? Nearly all do, need to, and should, but the specific sequences, criteria, and interdependencies are critical to the definition of a process. It is meaningless to call a process ADDIE if very different processes are called by the same name. Unfortunately, we're in such a state today, and it's unclear what people are really saying when they report use of ADDIE.

THE BEST MODEL

While there would be advantages to having a global, standard, highly effective ISD model, the best model today is the model that works well for an organization—one that assures each project will be completed within its constraints and will achieve desired performance outcomes to the fullest extent possible. Adaptation of models should be continuous as needs evolve and new best practices are recognized. But what might the foundation model be? Where should a team start?

Ideally, the numerous "new" versions of the ADDIE model could be seen as helpful efforts to move us closer to an effective model for creating engaging and effective learning. Unfortunately, it seems that many adaptations have been made because of challenges faced in implementing ADDIE (of which there are many) rather than to reach out directly for an improved process for quality learning design and development.

Adaptation of a familiar design approach is an understandable response by professionals in our field who need a realistic representation of their endeavors—a way to organize and communicate about what is happening. The more specific a model, the narrower its applicability. The more general a model, the more vague its clarity and utility.

"It appears that even instructional design models with some amount of utility must often be modified or adapted (even radically) by designers to render them applicable in context" (Yanchar, South, Williams, Wilson, 2007, pg. 1). The need to match the process to the environment in which the instruction is being developed demonstrates the inherent weakness of traditional design models for present-day design and development activities.

Suggesting that modified ADDIE processes allow teams to convey design options, evaluate approaches, and share ideas among the five phases of the model is too often just a theoretical notion and diversion from real and important process issues. Altering the sequence or connections of the five components of the ADDIE model may be a pointless task. Merrill asserts that the struggle for people offering adaptations of the ADDIE model components may derive from "the fact [that] their detailed implementation in various incarnations of ISD do not represent the most efficient or effective method for designing instruction" (2002, p. 39).

Experience in the complex work of instructional product development quite naturally gives rise to defined subtasks and procedures that become comfortable and routine. There is often a desire to "fix" the process while simultaneously clinging to the familiar aspects of it, whether they are truly productive or not. Focus turns to solving problems with the management of the process rather than to defining and sequencing tasks essential to creating great learning experiences. Spoken signs of clinging to the familiar at the sacrifice of producing great learning products include:

- *I have a form for subject matter experts to fill out, so I have on record what learners need to know. If it's wrong, it's wrong. I'm not a subject matter expert.*
- *I organize information into chunks readable in 15 minutes or less. I count the chunks, multiply by our average development time, and get the project timetable.*
- *Since people always want to make changes, I give them three "change for free" cards. Once they've used them up, no more changes. Don't even bring it up.*

- *Our modules never cover more than three objectives, and our quizzes always fit on a single page. It helps our designers to have defined spaces to write for.*
- *We figure each new project will require about three new templates in addition to our standard collection. After producing so many courses, we now have a fixed price for engineering new templates. So it's pretty easy to determine project costs now.*

While the basic concepts of the ADDIE model are essential to any effective design process, the approaches designers use are "far more varied and selective" and the processes are "much more heterogeneous and diverse than these ADDIE models suggest" (Visscher-Voerman and Gustafson, 2004, p. 70, 72) . Simply, these ADDIE models do not "address the complexity associated with instructional design" (Crawford, 2004, p. 418).

It seems then that it may be time to leave ADDIE behind. We've dragged it along with us for so many years in an adherence to the roots of ISD. We know its strengths and weaknesses, but we've adapted it and have the comfort of familiarity. Still, the results are not all they could be.

We want to stress once again, if the process you use meets your requirements and produces the quality product you want, you have the right process for you. We have seen ADDIE serve some organizations well. Typically, however, ADDIE appears to fall short. While ADDIE must be appreciated for what it's done in the past, let it no longer be the source of the boring and outdated instructional products it so often leads to. Let it no longer dictate a process that's simply too slow, laborious, and ineffectual. It's time to move on. Surely we can get comfortable with a new process once again.

CHAPTER 3

Anatomy of Effective Learning Events

It is impossible to define the best path to traverse if you don't know where you are going. While teams select a process based on attributes of the process itself, *Does it work for a small team? Is it hard to manage or learn? Does it produce products quickly enough?*, the only processes to consider are those that reliably produce the desired products. The desired product—whether as characterized here or otherwise—must be defined clearly to select a basic process and to optimize it for specific requirements.

This short chapter briefly explores some contemporary notions of ideal learning experiences and instructional design—not learning theory or instructional paradigms, per se, but rather the functional components needed to construct meaningful, memorable, and motivational learning experiences.

E-LEARNING BRINGS ISSUES TO LIGHT

Unfortunately, defining good learning events is more difficult than one would expect, as evidenced by the energetic debates on the topic that arise so frequently and also by the range of learning products organizations deem appropriate to use. Because e-learning implements instructional approaches in software that can be examined more clearly than the dynamics of instructor-led learning, e-learning seems to energize debates and controversies to a new level while also adding layers of complexity to the issues.

e-Learning forces critical issues to light and makes an excellent case study and proving ground for instructional product development processes because:

- Its instructional strategy must be explicitly defined in software.
- Unanticipated learner problems cannot be addressed.
- Each instructor cannot personalize to his or her own style and experience.
- Significant time and expense is involved.
- Learners have only the options provided.
- The proper role of computers in learning triggers concerns of dehumanizing a prized tradition of personal mentoring.

To build them, we need to be clear about what good learning events are, regardless of delivery means. While nuances are important, we need declared, readily understood fundamentals as a foundation. These fundamentals are divided into characteristics of what learning events must achieve and the primary components that create a learning event.

FUNDAMENTAL CHARACTERISTICS

Concise, effective learning events, whether delivered through e-learning or not, are meaningful, memorable, and motivational. And they achieve measurable results, too.

Meaningful

Meaningful learning events are those that assure learners can connect new content to their current knowledge and skills. They make sure learners recognize 1) how their current skills may not be sufficient in certain circumstances and 2) what tasks they will be able to perform after skill enhancement. Obviously, unfamiliar terms and concepts are not meaningful and impede learning, as does requiring use of skills not yet learned. We can only expect to change ineffective skills and performance by providing learners instruction that is grounded in their current understandings and abilities—preferably with a clear relationship to their real-world experiences.

Memorable

What good is instruction if it is not remembered when the need to perform arises? Good learning events provide learners the ability to perform effectively at the time of most value. Much is known amount about human memory and ways of helping people remember things, even though the complex capabilities of human memory continue to baffle scientists on many fronts. We know that distributed practice, for example, produces far greater retention than massed practice. We know that mnemonics can be useful aids, and we know that novelty can stimulate attention and make events more memorable.

Motivational

Motivated people find ways to learn what they need to learn to be successful. The hurdles they jump are proportional to their motivation, and while there may be a fair amount of time lost to trial and error and they may not learn best practices, motivated people learn. Lesser motivated people have a rougher time, since learning depends on what learners do—what they attend to, what they think about, what they practice. They may just complete the minimum of what is expected of them, if that, and move on, quickly forgetting whatever learning occurred. The good news is that motivation levels are fluid and can be nudged upward. The bad news is that they are just as easily nudged downward. To help learners learn, retain, and then apply their learning in real-world performance, effective learning events build on existing motivation and work to push it higher.

Measurable

Effective learning events produce skills that can be observed. Of course, we all have skills we don't use or don't use enough. We can't know easily if an individual has a skill and isn't applying it. But we shouldn't assume people have acquired skills when we can't observe their abilities. Learning is about performance skills, even if it's just to acquire the ability to carry out intelligent conversation on a topic. Teachers, employers, mentors, and clergy don't coach individuals so they can only know about desired performance. Their goal is to see people appraise situations accurately, determine the most effective course of action, and undertake it successfully. Therefore, good learning events stress observable behaviors, give learners sufficient practice, and provide performance feedback.

FUNDAMENTAL COMPONENTS OF INTERACTIVE LEARNING EVENTS

Humans have unique learning skills. One of them is our ability to learn simply from observation. Another is learning from just being told how to perform a task. Non-interactive learning events are effective when the following characteristics are met:

- The learner is familiar with most of the materials, tools, or concepts involved.
- The instructional presentation reveals steps and actions slowly and with clarity.
- The task to be learned has few steps and sequencing requirements.
- Characteristics of successful performance are understandable.
- There are no dangerous consequences of failures.

We learn many things from observation and imitation. We also learn many things from guidance, written and voiced instructions, and trial and error. One may well discover in the process of popping corn that preheating the oil produces a slightly crisper, better coated kernel and fewer unpopped kernels. Such unguided discovery is clearly a learning event.

When the goal is efficient learning of complex or challenging tasks, however, then a series of constructed learning events is often the best solution. And when many people need to reach the same or a minimum level of proficiency as quickly as possible, then instructional product development is in order.

A learning event occurs whenever learning happens, but for the purposes of this book, we are addressing those events that are created for the express purpose of helping others learn. We will address the creation of events for which materials are prepared, organized, and presented to help learners acquire skills efficiently.

Again, while nuances make huge differences, the foundational components of interactive learning events are context, challenge, activity, and feedback. The nature of these components and the ways in which they are interwoven define specific learning events. While not all of these components may be present in a specific learning event, we have observed that learning events are strongest when all four components are not only present, but also used in support of each other.

Context

Context is the relevant situation and conditions a learner must take into account when performing a task. It partially corresponds to the *conditions of performance* component of behavioral objectives as set forth by Mager (2004, p. 4). In implementation, we look not so much for a concise statement for learners to read as a situation to be presented, visualized if not illustrated, and perhaps explored. We want the context to become as vivid in the learner's mind as possible. Context can be portrayed by an instructor, augmented with media, or conveyed solely through e-learning media.

Examples of instructional context:

- A team of coworkers is reporting inability to complete a task because Sue refuses to compromise.
- An engine won't start after complete cool down.
- A remote railroad crossing has a high incident of fatal crashes.

Contexts are strong when they have relationships to real situations the learner will encounter, have fascinating attributes in them, and invite exploration for important but not so obvious details. The instructor can respond to questions to encourage such exploration, perhaps dropping hints, if necessary. Interactivity in e-learning can provide the means for learners to explore the context in as much depth as is relevant and productive.

In many ways, context is both the most foundational component and the most frequently neglected. When missing, it is much more difficult for learners to understand and remember the situations in which they should perform a task and why. As a result, learners can easily fail to recognize situations that require one response instead of another. They don't transfer their training into new situations or move to action unless familiar choices are presented. Without context, learners can be unsure of the personal relevance of the training to themselves. Enthusiasm and motivation decrease.

Context is critical for meaningfulness. It's why we say to a person who is not understanding us, *Let me put that in* context *for you.*

Challenge

Challenges spur learners to action and provide a wonderfully effective way of heightening motivation. Although distant challenges, such as end-of-course tests or even end-of-week quizzes can have some positive effects, it's unfortunate that challenges sit in wait while passive presentation activities consume so much of the time available for learning. Additionally, delayed and infrequent challenges can become unnecessarily frightening events, producing anxiety-fettered results.

Classroom settings hamper the ability to provide frequent challenges, especially when using a lecture format. Individuals can be called on to answer questions, of course, but this has the negative aspects of potential embarrassment. It is difficult, also, to challenge all individuals simultaneously, let alone at their individual levels of need. e-Learning has the advantage here, but only if the design avoids imitating the lecture format of presenting volumes of information followed by post-tests.

Effective challenges spur learners to re-examine the context and consider fully the probable outcomes of various responses. Just as in real life, we choose our responses based on previous experience and knowledge. We use the skills we presently have and, as we learn, modify them in hopes of achieving better results. Making mistakes and observing the consequences is a fundamental learning cycle, and by building challenges on relevant and authentic contexts, we enable this effective process.

Challenges must not be too difficult for learners, but neither is it effective to force learners through challenges that are boring because they are too simple. Good instruction adjusts challenges to match the individual's current level of progress. It also offers assistance to learners who request help or obviously need it.

Activity

If we're teaching our learners to do things, they need to be doing things while they are learning. In one-on-one mentorship, learners can swing a golf club, cut hair, or evaluate a subordinate's performance under close supervision. Experienced mentors give only a small amount of advice at first and then let learners try their hand while closely observing. They correct and advise with hesitation in hopes learners will fully apply themselves to the task rather than blankly waiting for direction. It's an effective approach when mentorship is practical, and it allows learners to approximate actual performance activity at the earliest possible moment.

> *If we're teaching our learners to do things, they need to be doing things while they are learning.*

Multiple-choice questions in the traditional "select a, b, c, or d" format contrast sharply from most authentic activities and nearly always focus on facts. *What part of the brain does…? Who was the first president to…?* Even when directed toward knowledge of processes, multiple-choice questions hardly assess any authentic activity because they provide a finite set of options to compare—options the learner might not have considered at all:

To make stiff but fluffy egg white peaks, you should (check all that apply):
- ☐ a. Use a copper bowl
- ☐ b. Be sure eggs are chilled
- ☐ c. Beat quickly at first and slow down as peaks begin to form
- ☐ d. Add an acid ingredient, such as cream of tartar

Multiple-choice questions are practical in terms of administration and scoring and are unfortunately commonplace in nearly all forms of instructional delivery except mentoring. The exception is revealing.

Reading about how to perform well is a preparatory activity, but answering a multiple-choice question about it is not an authentic activity. In contrast, facing a customer—simulated or real—who is expecting a stylish haircut, presents a performance challenge and activity that elevate the importance of the reading material to a critical level. The challenge motivates the learner. *What did it say about cutting tight curly hair?*

It's important to consider not only what activities are appropriate in an instructional event, but also where they best fit in the sequence. In many weakly designed learning events, listening or reading is the primary "activity," placed at the beginning of the event and consuming a high percentage of the total time. There are better places for this material. Effective activities look and feel to learners similar to the real tasks they expect to actually be performing post training.

Feedback

There are two primary types of feedback: consequences and judgments. *Consequences* reveal to learners what would really happen in response to their actions or inactions. Feedback in the form of consequences complements authentic activities to make the event as a whole feel realistic. If actual damages due to poor actions on the part of a learner are acceptable, the learning experience can move closer to the quality experience one might get with a good mentor who recognizes the value of mistakes and lets the learner witness the consequences of both correct and incorrect actions. Beginning learners need more support to avoid pointless floundering, but as they progress, corrective feedback should give way to feedback provided only through consequences (real or simulated).

Judgments appear in many forms, such as: "Correct." "No, you should chill the bowl before adding egg whites." "The correct answer is b." Judgments have their place, but in general they are more effective if delayed, so that learners have a chance to assess consequences and evaluate the effectiveness of their actions themselves. Judgments offered too quickly cheat learners of the opportunity to determine for themselves if they are making good choices and can lead to learner dependency on external assessment. In general, good instructional events offer consequences in the most realistic ways possible and put forth judgments only after it has become apparent that the learner needs direction.

Some learners will ask for help much more readily than others. Help should usually be given when requested, especially for beginning learners. In conjunction with consequences and judgments, challenge-based events should offer learners the comfort of ready access to relevant information and guidance. This doesn't mean that correct answers should be instantly available for the asking. When correct answers are easily exposed, many learners will instantly ask for them instead of fully engaging the challenge. Instead of revealing correct answers, support materials that lead to effective actions should be available, such as definitions, concepts, and worked examples.

CCAF Talk

Context, challenge, activity, feedback—CCAF. Discussing an instructional design in terms of CCAF helps to more clearly communicate an instructional paradigm. It's a functional way of talking with each other about instructional design that we have been so sorely lacking.

Infinite possibilities in instructional design arise from the countless combinations of variables and elements. While we have extraordinary flexibility and opportunities to invent new instructional paradigms, the number of considerations makes creating effective learning events a daunting challenge. And with such variability, it's been difficult to compare various approaches or even clearly define, understand, and communicate the nature of a single design.

While ADDIE has been shaped and reshaped into something of a cookbook recipe for developing instructional products, it has not firmly grappled with the challenge of defining instructional designs to be developed, implemented, and evaluated. Rather, it has sidestepped this difficult requirement that is actually prerequisite to the sequence of steps following its design phase (see Figure 2-1) and has focused on process details. Without clear communication of instructional designs, the success of the overall process is put at risk. The process too often misses the mark.

Viewing learning programs as a combination of contexts, challenges, activities, and feedback gives us a way of talking meaningfully about instructional products. Striving toward meaningful, memorable, and motivational learning events that produce measurable performance outcomes gives us the means of assessing the effectiveness of both products and the processes used to produce them.

With defined product components and desired product characteristics in hand, we are now ready to talk about process. What do we do when? How do we perform specific tasks?

CHAPTER 4

Successive Approximation Model 1

Almost every professional and academic team searches for a more effective model of designing and developing effective learning products. We're all working to find better ways of addressing the complex challenge that instructional product creation is.

Because each situation has different opportunities, constraints, and values, it's necessary to make adaptations unique to those requirements and to preferences as well. Teams hope, either openly or secretly, that their process will prove to have advantages over what everyone else is doing, allowing them to do more and better in less time. In many ways, this is part of the fun and reward of being a professional in a complex undertaking.

Before describing the successive approximation model, or "SAM," and listing its advantages, let's consider first the characteristics of an ideal process for designing and developing instructional products. Can there even be one, or should each team invent their own?

THE IDEAL PROCESS MODEL

Although for the inventive project manager there's a temptation to start from scratch, it's not necessary to bypass the considerable experience and wisdom gained from the millions of projects that have come before. History warns that frustration, late completion, and budget overruns are likely outcomes, even with an experienced team, when using many of today's traditional processes. Starting from scratch is a great idea when exploring processes, but not when trying to complete projects and honor commitments.

Indeed, while it seems that intuition should lead toward an effective process, one wouldn't consider such an approach for engineering a highway bridge. And while it may be a case of *my problems are tougher than yours,* many learning projects, especially those of significant size and those involving technology, are frightfully complex. When the team grows, with concomitant communication and coordination needs, problems snowball. Issues that may have been quickly and easily addressed by a couple of people become problems requiring meetings and much discussion.

We can learn by making mistakes. Giving learners an opportunity to make mistakes and see the consequences is an excellent instructional design strategy when there is little physical danger and when learners have the time necessary to make the mistakes and witness consequences. Typically, there isn't a lot of extra time to makes mistakes just to learn from consequences when tasked with putting out an instructional product. Although some mistakes will generate immediate feedback, some knowledge of results wouldn't come until learners were actually using the products. Then the cost of mistakes could be devastating.

Thankfully, we can also learn from the mistakes made and the successes achieved by others. From such mistakes—so many we've made personally and also mistakes we've recognized as we observed teams work—we recommend the following criteria for model selection.

Criterion #1 — The Process Must Be Iterative

A preferred process reveals as much about the developing product as early and continuously as possible. It allows frequent evaluation and course correction at times when corrections cost the least. It prevents investment of the majority of a project's time and budget before assessments can be made—before learners and stakeholders can get a clear picture of the product (see Figure 4-1).

Figure 4-1. Basic Iterative Process

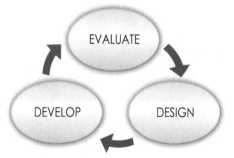

As opposed to a linear or waterfall process in which each step is done once, fully, and to the highest level of perfection possible (because subsequent steps build on previous steps), the iterative process takes small, somewhat experimental steps that can easily be reversed or modified several times.

Criterion #2 — The Process Must Support Collaboration

Although one-person design and development "teams" are common, others usually need to be involved. Learners, for example, while too frequently are not involved until a product has been nearly or fully finished, have much to offer and should be involved early and continually throughout the process.

Of course, there's no guarantee that a team of professionals, including sponsors, stakeholders, managers, and learners, will do better than a devoted and passionate individual. In fact, there's some evidence that individuals eventually produce superior products when given enough time. But it does take a single individual longer than a team, unless the team is poorly coordinated and managed. There are teams that seem almost totally unable to work effectively, whether through lack of leadership, clear process, deep differences of opinion, or other paralyzing factors. Coordinating expectations and roles can make the difference between success and failure when there are multiple team members and stakeholders.

An effective collaboration model is one that makes the most of the ideas, opinions, experiences, and knowledge of people with value to offer. It avoids bureaucracy and indecision that can cause projects to lose their way and waste precious time. It does this by being clear about who is doing what, when decisions are made and by whom, how the work is documented and communicated, and how the process flows.

Criterion #3 — The Process Must Be Efficient and Effective

Constraints always exist within which instructional products must be designed, constructed, and delivered. An effective process must work within constraints and also provide breathing room for addressing the unexpected issues that should always be expected.

No project is perfect or will ever become perfect. While the pursuit of perfection is a noble thought, it's a dangerous goal. The goal cannot be reached, but infinite time and money can be invested only to prove once again that perfection is like infinity itself; one can continually get closer but never arrive. With so many components in a course of instruction, there are many items to perfect. As one component changes, it may well require changes in other components. Attention skitters from one improvement to another while time passes too quickly, and yet perfection fails to arrive.

The selected model should therefore clarify where and when to focus energy and resources for maximum benefit. It should produce usable products as quickly as possible and allow time for improvements, even those identified late, that will significantly improve impact.

Perhaps most important is that the model produce the best learning experiences possible while staying within given constraints. We should reject a process that creates products with which no one wants to be associated.

Criterion #4 — The Process Must Be Manageable

One of the attractive attributes, perhaps even the most attractive attribute, of ADDIE is that it appears manageable. While evidence is lacking that ADDIE actually reduces cost and schedule overruns better than other processes, its defined phases and tasks make PERT chart production possible (see Figure 4-2). ADDIE PERT charts spanning 30 pages of tasks have been seen and offer impressive detail. Such charts are helpful to management (and everyone) because of the task requirements they reveal. And manageability is important.

Figure 4-2. Segment of a PERT Chart

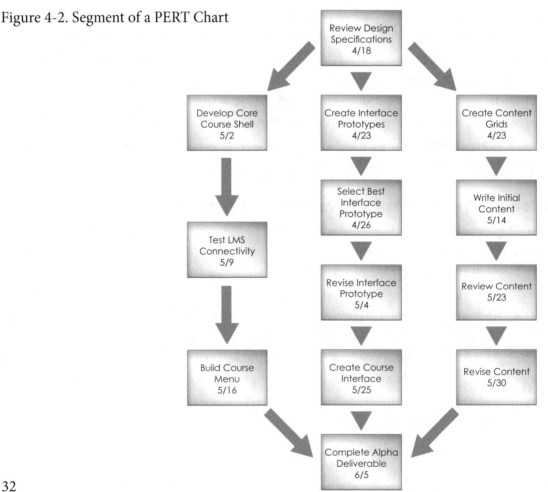

But while clarity is important to manageability, a process doesn't work well just because we can manage it. We must have both—a process that works and is manageable. And by manageable, we mean it's possible to complete projects within time and budget expectations, predict the impact of in-process changes, and produce a product that meets established criteria for quality.

So, there we have it—four primary criteria of an ideal process model: 1) iterative, 2) support for collaboration, 3) efficient and effective, 4) manageable. Let's see how successive approximation measures up.

SUCCESSIVE APPROXIMATION

The successive approximation model (SAM) provides a clear pathway to success, measurable and obtainable milestones for marking completion, and targeted moments to reach agreement and consensus. The model is clearly defined and manageable, and yet encourages creativity and experimentation. It consistently reveals the design as it evolves, and it does so in ways that all stakeholders can see and evaluate. It helps all team members communicate with each other, contribute, and collaborate. In short, it appears to meet all four criteria set forth above.

Level 1 (SAM1) Overview

A basic iterative process shown in Figure 4-3 is a very simple, but valuable and powerful version of SAM. It is very effective and well suited to smaller projects, especially when 1) an individual works alone or a small team of individuals works in unison and 2) no specialized skills such as software programming or video production require involvement of others.

Figure 4-3. Integrated Design and Development in SAM1

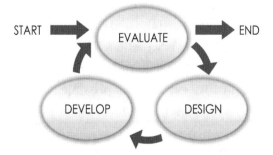

Iteration 1

The process repeats at least three times, starting and ending with evaluation. The initial evaluation looks at the situation, need, and alternative solutions. After each successive cycle of design and development, the emerging solution is evaluated to determine appropriateness and effectiveness. Information gathered in the initial evaluation is also re-examined for accuracy and sufficiency.

In the first iteration, design is kept to just listing objectives, sketching representative instructional treatments, and proposing methods to measure progress. Development is kept to preparing only representative content for each proposed delivery medium and instructional paradigm. Subsequent iterations will refine the work in terms of breadth, depth, and polish.

1. EVALUATE: Begin with a quick evaluation (analysis) of the situation, need, and goals.
- Who are the learners and what needs to change about their performance?
- What can they do now? Are we sure they can't already do what we want?
- What is unsatisfactory about current instructional programs, if any exist?
- Where do learners go for help?
- What forms of delivery are available to us?
- How will we know whether the new program is successful?
- What is the budget and schedule for project completion?
- What resources are available, human and otherwise?
- Who is the key decision maker and who will approve deliverables?

2. DESIGN: Quickly, but with thought, prepare a rough design for discussion.
- List and organize obvious goals.
- List behavioral objectives for each.
- List ways learner performance can be appraised.
- Select practical and appropriate delivery media.
- Sketch a few sample designs that appear to fit the situation and could reasonably be expected to achieve the goals. Be as visual as possible. (Sketching is an important activity we will return to in some detail later.)

3. DEVELOP: Prepare prototypes using whatever tools can quickly provide a sense of the design idea in application.

- Select representative content to flesh out some of the sketches. Just enough for understanding. "Tra, la, la…" should appear more often than carefully worded text.
- Stay in sketch mode; nothing fancy here. Prepare bullet points rather than paragraphs; use rough art, snapshots, and homemade video rather than illustrations, professional photos, and commercial video.
- Assemble props that instructors or learners might use to perform activities.
- Focus on prototyping learner activities instead of presentation content.

Iteration 2

The iterative process returns to evaluation, one notch up. On the next go around, it's time to:

1. EVALUATE: Determine the success of the first iteration.

- Was enough known about the situation, need, and goals? If not, it's time for some additional information gathering and analysis.
- What would and wouldn't work? Get some learners involved to help you decide. If instructors will deliver the instruction, conduct a mock class. Don't think it's too early.
- Where do alternatives need to be explored? Perhaps in this iteration, the team needs to sketch two or more alternative designs addressing the same content to compare.

2. DESIGN: Sketch new alternatives or refine previous ideas. If evaluation determines that the previous cycle should be repeated, it's important to do it. A cycle that clarifies needs or discards initial ideas is a success and an important step forward, but only if taken advantage of. Repeat Iteration 1 if needed. When it's time to move on:

- Force a new design. Try creating a design that does not incorporate the design from the first iteration. It may be hard and frustrating at first, but people nearly always find that by imposing the restriction of doing something different, they actually create something better—and something they wouldn't otherwise have created.
- Identify content that previous design(s) didn't accommodate well and create initial designs for them.
- Flesh out more thoroughly those ideas retained from previous iterations to be sure the designs can serve as a solid foundation. Representative content should be used, but it's not yet time to work with the full bulk of it. If there are different types of content, however, representative chunks should be chosen and the design expanded as necessary.

3. DEVELOP: Prototypes need to become more thoroughly representative of the final product.

- Prepare learner materials. Prepare a set of learner materials using a format close to the format under consideration for the final materials.
- Test delivery. Delivery means need to be tested soon, in either the next evaluation or the one in the cycle after that. The type of delivery determines the specific tasks.
  - If instructor-led delivery is planned, prepare instructor notes and support materials to a sufficient level that an instructor who has not been involved in the project could deliver a segment of instruction.
  - If using e-learning, prepare some interactive segments to test user interface designs and instructional approach.
  - If using distance learning, test compatibility of presentation materials and learner responses with the communications system.

Iteration 3

Iteration 3 is similar to Iteration 2, although as confidence builds that issues have been properly handled, issues must cease to be re-examined. The iterations become much more focused on development than design.

Additional iterations often seem attractive if not compelling, but if all content areas have been included in the first three, it's rare that additional iterations would return results worthy of the time and effort. It's usually much better to put the product in use, get experience with it, and then consider another round of improvements.

Evaluation of SAM1

SAM1 is quite simple, but nevertheless produces excellent products quickly. SAM1 is easy to manage because if work ever needed to be stopped unexpectedly or an emergency training need arose, the best product possible under the existing circumstances would be available for immediate use. Instead of having just a design specification, just storyboards, or just preparation for developing a product (as would be the case with other models), SAM1 produces something of a usable product after only a couple of quick iterations. Development work begins early in the process. This is done primarily to test ideas and assumptions, but it also provides instruction that is usable in an emergency. Early and continuous availability of a usable product is an outstanding advantage of this iterative approach.

SAM1 allows design correction early and frequently. It encourages creativity, but verifies ideas early enough to make changes if they fail to verify satisfactorily. It's a process that serves an individual well, but also facilitates teamwork and collaboration by making ideas tangible and concrete. Traditional processes rely on the approval of specification documents—approvals that are hard to win in a timely manner and yet are often given with divergent understandings of what is being proposed. Successive approximation shuns documentation in favor of prototypes that are much less easily misunderstood.

Reviewing the primary criteria above, this model does nicely here as well:
- ✓ iterative
- ✓ support for collaboration
- ✓ efficient and effective
- ✓ manageable

Challenges

There are challenges, of course, with every model. SAM is focused on process and is not a cookbook for instructional design. Instructional design can be difficult and often is. Knowledge of principles, experience, and talent are indispensable. While SAM1 helps less capable designers do a better job, there are two particular challenges even experienced designers may have trouble with:

1. **Refining work too soon.** Evaluation in the early cycles may indicate that a deeper understanding of the need is required, that the assumed delivery medium wasn't a good choice, or that different, more, or fewer people need to be taught. For the process to be nimble and self-correcting, it's very important that only enough effort is invested in design and development through the early cycles to determine if initial directions are valid and no more. In fact, it's best to assume that first decisions won't be valid and early design and development work will be discarded. If too much time and effort is put into early design and development, discarding it will be painful rather than seen as a very important step forward. Poor choices are often adhered to because too much time and effort was invested too early in the process.

2. **Perpetual cycling.** There's always a better idea. In fact, as projects progress, the quantity of better ideas tends to rise rather than decrease. Insights and ideas get better and better, while discontent with the chosen direction also increases. Repetition, familiarity, exhaustion, or boredom can lead to making changes simply to refresh the project.

    Time will eventually run out, and excessive fine-tuning can endanger completion. Implementing just one more great idea can delay rollout. And there's always one more great idea, *just one more*. But it would often be better to stop, reserve any remaining time and budget for making improvements later, roll out the product, and gain experience with learners. Most likely, the great ideas that just couldn't wait will be upstaged by much better ideas gleaned from real application.

That's It?

SAM1 is a simple concept. It has something of a "just do it" attitude, favoring action that results in a tangible product to review. While nearly every task prescribed by ADDIE and traditional ISD models is performed in SAM1, they are less onerous and more productive in SAM1. Tasks are short and strive less for perfection. If there is enough to go on, there is enough. There's no need to write a longer paper, collect more data, have more meetings. If there isn't enough to go on, the situation is not only discovered quickly, but the need is also clarified in context so that the right amount of effort can be put to it.

SAM1 is a deceptively simple concept. The apparent simplicity of the model might suggest there is little to it, yet that's not the case; there's careful work to be done and pitfalls to avoid. Helpful, however, is that the work does not so much serve the model as the model serves the work—assuring each step is productive and everyone remains aware of where the work is heading.

CHAPTER 5
Successive Approximation Model 2

The second successive approximation model, SAM2, is an elaborated and extended version of SAM1 for situations in which development cannot be fully integrated with design. While there are many advantages to fully integrating design and development into a single cycle as is done in SAM1, it isn't always practical. Projects with large amounts of content, e-learning projects developed through programming rather than with quicker authoring tools, and organizations that need to begin development production only after design has been completed (such as when development is contracted out), are examples of when SAM2 may be needed.

Work in SAM2 is divided into three phases: preparation, iterative design, and iterative development. A brief overview of the process begins on the next page (see Figure 5-1). In subsequent chapters and the remainder of the book we will discuss and review the activities and milestones that occur throughout the three phases of the SAM2 process.

Figure 5-1. Overview of SAM2

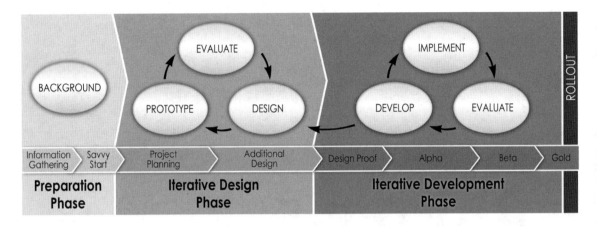

As with SAM1, SAM2 depends on functional prototype development within design iterations. But SAM2 prescribes separate iteration cycles for development (from which design issues may arise, triggering the need for additional design work—note the return arrow from development phase to design phase in Figure 5-1).

PREPARATION PHASE

The preparation phase is the period for gathering background information before attempting to design the first solution. Backgrounding helps set the target, identify special issues, and rule out options. It prepares for the intensive design activities in the next phase by narrowing focus. This is the time for actively exploring the performance problem in broad terms—its context within the organization's needs, goals, and outcome expectations.

Background information to be gathered includes:
- previous performance improvement efforts (if any) and their outcomes
- programs currently in use (if any)
- available content materials
- organizational responsibilities for training
- constraints, such as schedule, budget, and legal requirements
- who is the ultimate decision maker
- what will define project success.

Key backgrounding objectives:

- Identification of the key players and their commitment to participate. Key players include: decision and budget maker, opportunity owner, subject expert, performance supervisor, recent learner, target learner, and organization's deployment manager.
- Identification of the organization's primary opportunity here and its dependency on specific behavioral changes.

In SAM, preparation work is done quickly at first, taking paths of least resistance. It's not because this work is unimportant—it's critically important to base decisions on accurate information and avoid the risk of making unverified assumptions, but the model prescribes performing analysis in the context of considering alternative solutions. It explicitly avoids exhaustive research that will be inevitably incomplete anyway and might not even prove useful.

At the start of the process, much time can be spent collecting information that could be relevant, but turns out not to be very helpful. We need to get to the right questions to research—quickly. Perhaps it's surprising, but identifying the right questions comes partly from the iterative design phase where the context of the questions makes them more specific.

Perhaps the clearest way to state this important concept is this: Most of the analysis work will be addressing the question, *"Why isn't this design a good solution?"* rather than the question, *"What are all the possible solutions?"* But before we start designing, if there are obvious things to avoid and obvious considerations to include, there's no reason to begin blindly. So we collect the information that's readily available and move on to the Savvy Start.

Savvy Start

The *Savvy Start* is a solutions brainstorming event in which the design team and key stakeholders review collected background information and generate initial design ideas. This phase of the design process begins with jumping into solutions stakeholders may already have in mind. While it's important to get these on the table as soon as possible, whether they are destined to become part of the final solution or eventually abandoned, this activity proves invaluable for many purposes, not the least of which is determining who is really in charge and what outcomes are essential to success. Brainstorming solutions is an amazingly efficient way of determining what the main performance objectives are and simultaneously dealing with the organization's hierarchy that can so easily obscure understanding needs and goals.

Further information is discovered by design and review of rapidly constructed, disposable prototypes. These prototypes promote brainstorming and creative problem solving, help the team determine what really is and isn't important, and help align the team's values.

Savvy Start highlights:
- Design cycles are used to evaluate the direction suggested by gathered information, assumptions, and early ideas.
- Prototypes are very rough and finished just barely enough to communicate and test ideas.
- Outcome performance objectives are listed along with the prototyped designs that will be used to help learners achieve them.
- Evaluation is done merely by discussion. Redefining and changing everything may be appropriate, including even the business problem to be addressed and the people to be trained.
- Rapid is the key!

ITERATIVE DESIGN PHASE

As in SAM1, design, prototyping, and evaluation are done iteratively in small steps. The major difference is that in SAM2, the project moves on to the development phase when design iterations have been completed, whereas in SAM1 the product is completed at the conclusion of these iterations (see Figure 5-2).

Figure 5-2. Iterative Design Phase of SAM2

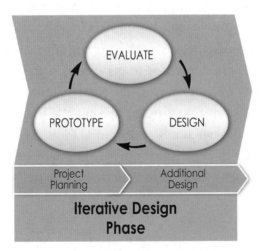

With larger projects or teams, documentation and coordination are prerequisites to success. Note the additional activities along the bottom of the model diagram (Figure 5-2). Described in more detail below, the Savvy Start is an orchestrated brainstorming session in which rapid-fire iterations of evaluate-design-prototype cycles are completed. Project planning identifies tasks and who will hold responsibilities for them. Additional design is produced later through more iterations, but by a smaller team focused on covering additional content, resolving inconsistencies among designs, or solving problems that arose along the way. These later design needs may actually be identified in the development phase as issues or opportunities are discovered.

Project Planning

Project planning involves quantitative assessment of remaining project development details affecting timeline and budget. It involves careful consideration not only of cost and quality management, but also of related communication, risk, schedule, scope, and staffing implications.

Project planning highlights:
- Based on the designs created or selected in the Savvy Start, it's now possible to create a project plan that has integrity.
- The first step is to capture discussions and decisions by preparing and circulating a *Savvy Start Summary Report*.
- Initial *Media and Content Style Guides* can also be prepared, although they are likely to be incomplete until additional design cycles have been completed (see below). It's easy and efficient to capture preferences as they spill out.
- An initial draft of a *Content Development Plan* can be prepared, indicating responsibilities and estimates of what material will be needed.
- Content writing, media development, and programming can now be estimated for the overall project plan.
- The biggest risk lies with learning and performance objectives for which no solutions have yet been prototyped. There are likely to be some.

Additional Design

The Savvy Start session may take only a half-day, three full days, or sometimes even more. The length is as often determined by incidental factors, such as availability of people or meeting space, as it is by project parameters, such as quantity and complexity of content or variation in learner readiness. As intense (and fun) as these sessions often are and should be, they are more properly considered brainstorming sessions rather than design sessions.

Good ideas and preferences spill out, the need for research and more information becomes apparent, and attractive instructional approaches emerge that need to be thoughtfully reviewed and refined, if not modified extensively or even replaced on closer examination. Further, while the involvement of key stakeholders is essential to truly understanding boundaries and expectations, these people usually can't afford the time necessary to reach needed depth or cover all the content. Additional design work will be needed.

The additional design team will likely be smaller, and team members will likely be charged with preparing ideas in advance of meeting with others. It remains important, however, to follow the rule of *breadth before depth*. That is, it's important to consider all the content to understand whether a broad variety of instructional treatments will be necessary, or whether just one or a few will be appropriate for all content. With each iteration, design can become more specific and reach greater depth until all details are finalized.

Prototypes

Prototypes continue to be important to test and communicate ideas. A usable prototype is better than any description, specification, or storyboard. A prototype communicates specificity by example, making it easy for people to understand, ask questions, and make detailed comments. Multiple types of prototypes may be developed following the Savvy Start depending on the selected means of delivery.

Media prototypes integrate media elements to demonstrate the desired "look-and-feel." Layout, colors, fonts, images, and samples of other elements are brought together to form a clear design example and set criteria for full product development.

Functional prototypes are usually derived from Savvy Start prototypes by enhancing or adding details to make them testable with learners. In the case of e-learning, increased functionality provides a better sense of interactivity and usability.

Integrated prototypes present the integration of functional and media prototypes along with representative content (i.e., feedback text, sound, video, and so on).

Special-purpose prototypes are created to test any technical or design components that must be finalized early in the process.

Additional design highlights:

- The same iterative process of design—prototype—evaluate is used following the post–Savvy Start. The key decision makers should review and approve the new prototypes before development commences. Trusting they will be happy with how things are evolving is not a good practice.

- Except for small projects and those with a very narrow focus, there isn't enough time to create functional prototypes for all behavioral objectives. It's therefore important to review all content and organize it by similarities so that the smallest number of necessary treatments and prototypes can be identified. You need a prototype for each type of content, but not for each instance of the same type of content.

- Post–Savvy Start prototypes can be created with a smaller team and, as is often necessary, even without some of the key people, although their participation is always preferred. Again, if key people are not involved, it's not safe to proceed without getting their approval. A surprise objection late in the process can be devastating.

ITERATIVE DEVELOPMENT PHASE

The iterations that are so advantageous to the design process are equally powerful for development activities. They allow stakeholders to continue to have a means of evaluating decisions and making corrections within project constraints. The importance of this advantage cannot be overstated. Because a functional product becomes available quickly, before time-consuming refinements are made, stakeholders can get an invaluable glimpse of the design becoming real (see Figure 5-3).

Figure 5-3. Iterative Development Phase

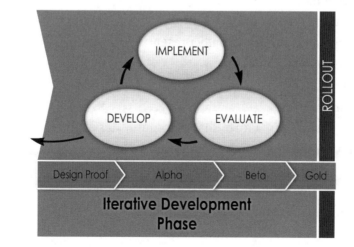

Design Proof

At the beginning of the development phase, a plan is made to produce a *design proof,* which is typically the product of the first cycle. Projects with large amounts of content will require a cycle for each type of instructional approach. Approval or disapproval will determine whether:

- Additional design work or design rework is needed. If so, the process returns to iterative design to produce needed designs.
- Another development iteration is needed to make corrections.
- Iterative development can proceed to producing an *alpha* version of the final product.

The design proof is essentially a visual, functional demonstration of the proposed solution that integrates samples of all components to test and prove viability. It has greater functionality or usability than the design prototypes and is built with the same tools that will produce the final deliverable. In this way, it not only tests the viability of the design, but also of the production system.

If technology is involved, the design proof needs to run on the equipment and network to be used by learners and demonstrate functional communication with the learning management system, if one is to be used.

Design proof evaluation is a critical event in the process. Design proofs are used to scout out potential problems so they don't become last-minute crises. It's the big opportunity for the design team and the stakeholders to check how the course will function as a whole. At this point, it is possible to get the clearest sense of what the overall solution is becoming while still having time to note corrections that are clearly needed.

Design proof highlights:
- The first production cycle produces the design proof, which provides an opportunity to confirm all design decisions by actually presenting and testing a functional application on the intended delivery platform.
- Design proofs test:
  - design viability
  - whether the design is in a form that communicates requirements effectively
  - the suitability of development tools and processes.
- Design proofs combine sample content, including examples of all components, with design treatments. Text and media are polished and representative of the final quality to be expected for all similar elements.

Alpha

The alpha is a complete version of the instructional application to be validated against the approved design. All content and media are implemented. If problems exist, and they well might because it is often important to begin evaluation before all issues can be rectified, those known problems are listed. No major, undocumented issues are expected to be found, but it's nevertheless common for them to surface despite everyone's best efforts.

Evaluation of the alpha release identifies deviations from style guides, graphical errors, text changes, sequencing problems, missing content, lack of clarity, and functional problems.

Alpha highlights:
- The second production cycle (or set of cycles for large projects) produces the alpha from approved designs.
- Full content development integration occurs in this cycle. Samples no longer suffice.
- The alpha is nearly the final version of the complete instructional program to be validated against the approved design. All content and media are implemented.
- Completion and approval of the alpha signals the beginning of the validation cycles.
- Review of the alpha is expected to find only minor deviations from style guides, writing issues, graphical errors, and functional problems.

Beta

Because errors are nearly always found in alpha releases, a second cycle, called the validation cycle, is scheduled as part of the process to produce a second final product candidate, the beta release. The beta is a modified version of the alpha that incorporates needed changes identified during evaluation of the alpha. If all goes as expected and corrections are made carefully, the beta review should discover few errors, and those errors discovered should include only minor typographical errors, or corrections in graphics.

Beta highlights:
- The alpha release is modified to reflect errors identified in its evaluation. The resulting beta release is viewed as a first gold release candidate. There should be no functional errors at this stage.
- The beta release should be evaluated by not only subject matter experts, but also by actual learners representative of the target population.

Gold

Construction of the gold release is the final phase of development. At this point, while no project ever reaches perfection, the courseware becomes fully usable within the parameters of previously approved project guidelines.

Gold release highlights:
- If problems are identified, they must be rectified before the beta release can be given the gold crown. A modified version of a beta, "beta 2" (sometimes called "gold candidate 2") and, if necessary, a succession of numbered candidates is produced until all problems are resolved.
- When the beta performs as expected and no additional problems are identified, it simply becomes the gold release without further development and is ready for rollout implementation.
- Hopefully, but all too rarely, rollout signals the beginning of an evaluation study to determine whether targeted behaviors are actually achieved and whether these new behaviors secure the performance success expected.

CHAPTER 6

Are You The One?

You may have been asked to create instructional materials or you may expect to do so soon. You may be leading a development effort that someone else (your school, your boss, the manager of another department, or a colleague) has requested. You may be ultimately responsible for communicating the success, struggles, alternatives, and completion of the training solution. If you are, this makes others the "client" and you the project leader.

It's often assumed that the instructional designer will take the initial training goal and just make training happen. Underestimating this complex task can easily lead to unfulfilled expectations, ineffective design, and off-budget and off-schedule projects.

It is essential to the success of your project that you are able to constructively discuss timelines, budget, treatment alternatives, and review and approval obligations with your client (even if they aren't paying you as a consultant). Setting and maintaining clear expectations with the project sponsor (client) throughout the project ensures that there will be few surprises on either side.

Keeping the client informed as to the status of the project is not enough. You could accomplish that as a project manager. You need to be a consultant. The difference between a consultant and a project manager is your skill in identifying and presenting alternatives, setting and maintaining expectations, building and leading the team, and effectively negotiating with everyone involved throughout the whole project. An iterative process is all about alternatives—to the design, media, strategies, timeline, budget, and more.

Successive approximation gives you the means to produce highly effective learning, on budget and on schedule, through collaborative teamwork, small iterative steps, and continuous course correction. It's a very successful process, but it's essential to adhere to the rules of the process. Success therefore lies in the ability of the project leader to manage all of the project flow effectively.

The leader must be a dynamic in-line manager of the process and able to adjust the activities, design, and project variables without losing project momentum. If adjustments cause the project to stall or move backward, the work up to that point, and the faith that the project can be successful, may be at risk. Fortunately, those problems are far more prevalent in traditional ISD than with SAM. Perhaps the most pressing leadership skills are confidence in the process and the ability to win support for it from all participants.

There will be calls for exceptions and violations of the process to resist or at least negotiate. It's very easy to pursue too much perfection too early—to strive for too much before product rollout. So, as a SAM leader, you must prepare to:

- set and maintain expectations
- dynamically adjust design and project variables
- resist superfluous modifications
- combat indecision
- keep the focus on behavior change
- be an advocate for the learner.

SETTING AND MAINTAINING EXPECTATIONS

The fundamental question that all clients have is "When will it be done?" Although you have a clear schedule and the team is fully committed, you should expect that there will be some pressure on the schedule that must be communicated to the client. A content expert may not be available, media may have to be rebuilt, your instructional writer may take vacation at the worst time, or someone could have an unexpected emergency. Conservative planning with built-in contingencies can help manage assaults on the schedule, but it's common that the client both causes delays and becomes upset with you about them.

You should always be considering creative solutions to any problem that may arise in the project. But you will need to be just as creative in your communication of schedule conflicts as of your solutions. The client may have expectations for *how* things are handled as much as *when* they are handled. Make sure you are aware of their expectations.

DYNAMICALLY ADJUSTING DESIGN AND PROJECT VARIABLES

As the project leader, you are charged with producing an instructional product that meets the expectations of management, the sponsor, team members, learners and their managers, all while producing desired behavior changes. There's a lot that goes into a successful project, not to mention your ability to juggle them all.

There is no more important skill for an effective SAM leader than the ability to effectively negotiate. This is even more important if the client has not been involved in the early stages of the design process (but hopefully you would not have let that happen).

Instructional negotiation involves identifying opportunities and alternatives to the design that either improve the instructional treatment or address an ineffective treatment, then gaining agreement with the project sponsor, stakeholders, and the team members.

Negotiation requires trade-offs and compromises. Additional development, content, or media are often seen as required improvements even though they necessitate more time and budget than exist in the plan. As the SAM leader, you need to point out that no schedule or budget allows perfection, and it would be better to rollout a product with some resources in reserve should quick fixes be needed, than to delay release and have no means to make corrections later. Actual use of a product should be considered just another cycle of evaluation leading to future design and development. This is far more effective and efficient than trying to guess what the real world response will be. So you should challenge "simple fixes" and remind people of the advantages of the process they agreed to at the beginning.

In many cases, you'll have to do something you didn't anticipate. Your role will be to come up with practical solutions. Maybe providing a link to a policy document or to an existing course can fix the perceived problem. Maybe an activity addresses a topic that is somewhat outside the scope of the project and should be moved to a separate course rather than being enhanced. Maybe a previous design option that was prototyped and discarded should be revisited.

These choices require someone who understands the options and their impact on the project and can communicate them to the project owner. By striving to be an effective consultant and sticking to the SAM process, you can shepherd your project through tough challenges and negotiate with confidence.

KEEPING THE FOCUS ON BEHAVIOR CHANGE

The role of an instructional designer is to focus on instructional events that achieve learning goals and objectives. The role of the project manager is to focus on the budget, team activities, and timelines. The role of the media artist is to design and create visual treatments and objects to support the course content. The role of the developer is to construct components that bring the course design to life.

All of these roles are essential in the development of good instruction, but they only represent the means to constructing it. A project leader needs to ensure that each constructed piece or component works to address the behavior change that was identified in the Savvy Start. The leader's role is to make certain that design, budget, and timeline decisions continue to focus on changing learner performance.

BEING A LEARNER ADVOCATE

It is hard to believe that someone would build a course of instruction with a malicious attitude toward learners. Nonetheless, the realities of the project (finding the budget, staying on schedule, keeping team members on task, and so on) easily shift the focus of the team away from the true needs of the learners. Defocusing project pressures are nearly constant, while learner considerations may have little advocacy.

The SAM leader needs to be the one to take a step back and see the learner standing behind the spreadsheets, plans, drafts, and schedules. A learner-centered approach means challenging the design via learner review and feedback, as well as reiterating the identified learner expectations identified in the Savvy Start. An effective leader should be an unfaltering advocate for learners throughout the project.

ARE YOU A SAM LEADER?

A checklist of skills helpful for SAM leadership appears below. This checklist is divided into four specific areas necessary for anyone who endeavors to lead a successful project: instructional design, project management, consulting, and selling.

SAM LEADERSHIP PREPAREDNESS CHECKLIST	Not True			True	
	1	2	3	4	5
Instructional Design					
1. I am knowledgeable about the fundamental components of good instructional design.					
2. I am capable of designing creative instructional treatments.					
3. I am capable of identifying the key objectives of the instruction.					
4. I understand how one component of our ISD process relates to and affects the other components.					

SAM LEADERSHIP PREPAREDNESS CHECKLIST	Not True			True	
	1	2	3	4	5
Project Management					
1. I can create and plan an effective project schedule.					
2. I understand how to use project resources to make the project successful.					
3. I am comfortable with handling schedule shifts.					
4. I am able to communicate the progress of the project clearly and confidently.					
5. I am skilled at keeping project team members on task and on schedule.					
Consulting					
1. I am comfortable explaining my process to others.					
2. I am able to understand client concerns and the reasons for them.					
3. I am confident recommending a course of action or approach.					
4. I can adjust my plan of action to accommodate a client's concerns or wishes.					
5. I can help the client visualize the approaches and treatments under consideration.					
6. I am able to discuss the pros and cons of the approach or treatment that is recommended.					
7. I know and can identify the difference between a learner-centered design and a content-centered design.					
Selling					
1. I am successful at persuading others.					
2. I am able to encourage clients to discuss their real needs.					
3. I can convince clients of what's important and what's not.					
4. I am able to connect with my client on a personal and professional level.					

PART II

Using the Successive Approximation Model

When used by teams to develop courses of instruction, the successive approximation model (SAM) has an uncanny ability to both foster creative designs and manage the work to fit time and cost constraints. Perhaps the most important advantage of SAM is its ability to simultaneously reach these two often-conflicting goals.

Part II provides a more detailed look at successive approximation in application for the design and development of larger projects. Because SAM is commonly used to handle the complexities of e-learning, we give some special attention to its use for e-learning design and development; however, SAM is of great advantage for designing and developing all forms of instructional delivery, simple to complex, technology-assisted or not.

CHAPTER 7

Preparation Phase

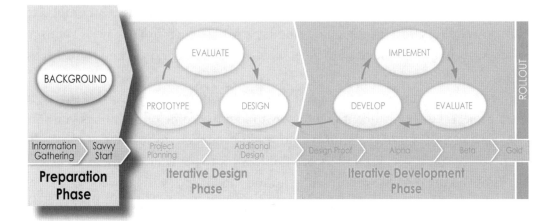

The preparation phase gets things going quickly. The philosophy of "just do it" doesn't fully capture the spirit of successive approximation, although it's close in many ways. We want to get into the consideration of alternatives as a means of research rather than exhaustively studying the situation, writing reports, and still not having a clear idea of what would be best to do (although from all the time and effort spent, exhaustive efforts may make it feel like the path is clear and ready for paving even when it isn't). We do want to:

- gather knowledge of the situation to understand challenges
- be aware of opportunities
- eliminate consideration of unviable paths
- enable everyone to be a constructive brainstormer.

After gathering information, we launch the Savvy Start, where the team begins iteratively proposing and evaluating alternative design ideas.

Let's get to the details.

BACKGROUNDING

The preparation phase begins with collection of background information about the project that will guide design and delivery decisions. But there is no need, for example, to replicate efforts that have failed in the past and no need to develop courseware for delivery by experts if expert instructors are not available. But, there may be an opportunity to complement commercially available materials rather than develop everything from scratch. It's easy to make poor assumptions that thwart success or make solutions unnecessarily complicated.

The backgrounding effort asks such questions as: what's been done, who is sponsoring the project, who is the intended audience, what information exists, and who needs to be involved.

Of course, at this time one could never collect all of the information needed to successfully complete a project. Further, while it's quite easy to identify some of the things you should know, you can't identify all of the information you'll need. You don't know what you don't know. But, not to worry, backgrounders need only work to get what information is readily available, knowing the process will present questions and help reveal answers.

At the start, we complete a thorough gathering of the background information that currently exists and is readily available. We take a nice starting bite, then see where it leads. Later, in iterative evaluations, you'll know what information is worth some effort to gather and study. Perhaps Allison Rossett puts it best: "I'm proposing that we reduce the daunting size of the effort by carving the planning process into more manageable and iterative bite sizes: one swift, targeted bite up front and then subsequent mouthfuls of assessment for subsequent associated programs" (1999, p. 4).

Make no mistake. Backgrounding is a very important task. Someone has decided this project is necessary and needed. An effective review of background information will ensure the team is fully aware of the direction of the project and the expectations for it. Expectations will change, perhaps as a result of learning about unforeseen options, but it will save a lot of time to know what the starting expectations are.

Initial Information You Need to Know

Some of the most helpful information to have initially is:

- Who is sponsoring the project (i.e. has budget authority)?
- Who cares most about success?
- Why is a learning program being developed now?
- What behaviors need to change or what skills need to be developed?
- Who is the intended audience?
- What continuing performance support will learners have?
- How often will learners perform the tasks they are learning to perform?
- What delivery means can be used? (For example, instructors, self-study, remote, e-learning, and so on.)
- What's been tried in the past? What were the results?
- What content currently exists, and what form is it in?
- Is the budget preset? If so, what is the maximum that can be invested?
- Is there a critical rollout date? When? Are there advantages to early completion?
- Who needs to be involved?
- Who is available to help? (For example, content experts, supervisors, learners, media artists, writers, or reviewers.)

Gathering Information

People may not be aware of what might be extremely useful. So it's smart to ask for guides, manuals, PowerPoint presentations, instructor notes, and opportunities to talk briefly with learners, their supervisors, trainers, and subject matter experts. If it makes sense, ask to observe people performing behaviors to be taught. Learn about organizational values and initiatives that could be reinforced or used to establish relevance of the instruction. Right now, finding out who has answers may be more important than having the answers.

A good place to start gathering information is with the project sponsor. What does this person regard to be the performance gap or learning need? This perception will cast creative discussions in the kick-off meeting. In interaction with the sponsor, it's most important to assess the level of involvement the sponsor wants to have and to itemize every expectation, such as use of media, humor, learning games, and so on. How will the sponsor determine if the project is successful? Would the sponsor like to be involved in brainstorming or look at some early prototypes?

The performance need of an organization often dictates who the group of learners will be, but logical as it is, this can lead to erroneous assumptions. Supervisor training, for example, is often overlooked, as are possibilities that better tools, communication, or incentives could provide desired performance more effectively.

It's important to determine the current constraints for the project (budget and timeline, among others). This information will help scope efforts during and after the kick-off meeting. The project sponsor may want to change the world, but will only allow three months in which to do it. The team will want to know this success factor early!

THE SAVVY START

The Savvy Start has so many vital purposes and makes so many contributions to the activities that follow, it's hard to identify them all. One of the most important purposes is to answer the fundamental questions: What will it cost to train our people? How long will it take to develop the training?

What will it cost to train our people? How long will it take to develop the training?

These questions are often the initial questions asked long before any analysis has been done. Sometimes they are answered in a budget meeting where people just enter an amount that seems reasonable to them. The budget amount is rarely looked at as a percentage of what will be saved or of the possible earning increases; it's just a number based partly on history and partly on how much works comfortably with other allocations.

A learning professional is often asked these questions with pressure added to answer without any analysis. A common plea might be: *I understand the concerns. Of course there's a lot to consider. But you've developed a lot of training. Just tell me what would be a good budget—a ballpark estimate.* The Savvy Start is an informed and responsible way to go about estimating appropriate approaches, time, budget, and resources. Some projects are over-funded through ballpark estimates and many more should not even have been attempted because the estimate was far too restrictive to produce results.

As the theory of iterative, prototype-based design has become practice, we have learned the importance of recognizing and managing organizational issues that affect process (any process) and decisions. It's important for designers to know, for example, that the organization and its leaders place a high value on certain media. One large organization I worked with stated quite matter-of-factly to me, "About two-thirds of our training needs to be delivered via video. It will be boring and ineffective otherwise." They felt this was true regardless of the subject and the skills being learned. While video can be powerful, it can also be boring and ineffective. There are many considerations. But knowing early about strongly held values and preconceptions can help the design team be more successful with the organization and able to address issues at the best times.

The Savvy Start assembles key players together to prevent having to run between them individually to carry messages and get consensus. It allows designers to see who is actually in charge and most influential and perhaps most difficult to please. It clarifies what will be considered the key measures of success. It provides an opportunity to get stakeholder expectations in-line with each other. And it provides an opportunity for stakeholders to consider alternative approaches that might not have been obvious. Enthusiasm for an approach conceived through collaboration is a terrific way to start any project.

The activity of the Savvy Start is basically SAM1 in rapid motion (see Figure 7-1). There will be repeated efforts to 1) evaluate the situation, 2) design a possible learning activity, and 3) develop (prototype in this case) the design for evaluation. The type of development possible in this rapid motion context depends on the design and tools the team is using. To serve the needs, it has to be fast.

Figure 7-1. Integrated Design and Development in SAM1

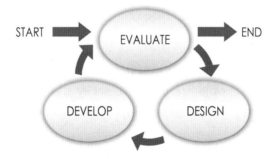

The Savvy Start is a unique type of meeting combining creative brainstorming, prototyping, planning, revising, and storytelling. This meeting is more than just a celebration of a project start; it takes specific steps to reach preset goals. These steps have to be executed rapidly, which requires organization and preparation. We will detail the components of the Savvy Start later, but we turn first to planning the event. Just getting key people together without careful preparation will not serve the purpose of this key event.

PLANNING THE SAVVY START

Preparation for a Savvy Start requires:

- gathering background information
- creating a Savvy Start team and setting expectations
- creating an agenda
- preparing the room and gathering materials.

Brainstorming, storytelling, and prototyping take some time, and that's why teams should schedule two to three days for the Savvy Start. These should be consecutive days. Even though it may be hard to get everyone to commit to that much time out of his or her office, it is important and necessary. Creative momentum is important, and spreading this meeting over a couple of weeks would make it difficult to keep the momentum. It would add time to the project schedule.

Since people will be in a room with six (or more) others for a few days, a comfortable and spacious room can contribute to an effective outcome. Although many Savvy Starts have been completed in cramped rooms, it's not a recommended strategy. Somewhere out of the office, such as a hotel conference center, is preferable to being close to offices where people do not detach from their daily routines and responsibilities. This meeting is a crucial first step, and it deserves proper attention, commitment, and involvement.

BUILDING A SAVVY START TEAM

Picking the right people to be on the team and in the Savvy Start might not be as easy and obvious as it appears. The right people are not necessarily the ones who understand the content, but are people who can provide ideas, support, information, direction, creativity, and possibly inspiration.

Subject matter experts (SMEs) are very helpful when specific information is needed, but they may not have experience with learners or the awareness of the environment where the performance occurs. More importantly, SMEs are often too close to the information to be creative in the design of effective interactive instructional treatments. But the project needs to have accurate content, of course. A team of blank stares is a dead end when the question arises of what needs to be taught. It's less a question of whether an SME should attend, than of which SME should attend.

Table 7-1 provides a list of potential candidates and the reason for selecting them for your project design team.

Table 7-1. Roles and Responsibilities on the Savvy Start Team

Role	Example Responsibilities
Budget maker	This person can explain budgetary constraints, know the budget will be (or was) set, and assumptions made.
Person who owns the performance problem	This person will help to determine the organization's expectations for successful performance.
Person who supervises performers	Supervisors are closest to the real performance issues and will provide the most concrete examples of the performance problems that need to be solved.
Someone who knows the content (SME)	This person can provide insight into the content and direction for the instruction.
Potential learners	These people will support the ongoing development of the course through user testing and review.
Recent learners	Recent learners will help the team understand the strengths and weaknesses of current instruction, what is easy and hard to learn, and what may be best to learn on the job.
Project manager	This person will manage all of the resources and schedules on the project.
Instructional designer	Designer(s) will select or create instructional treatments and keep the instruction focused on the learner.
A prototyper	This person will sketch and/or build prototypes to give the team the opportunity to visualize the team's ideas.

There are more people to consider, such as the person who:
- is responsible for maintaining the brand standards
- handles HR and legal activities
- will ensure the course is deliverable in the environment (availability of A/V equipment, compatible network, etc.).

The support and guidance from these important people will be needed later in the project. Involving them at the start of the project can ease resolution of problems later on, but whether to invite them or not is not an easy decision.

The team needs to be fully engaged during design brainstorming sessions. The primary goal of marketing, HR, legal, and IT departments of corporate organizations will not (and should not) be to dream up interactive instructional treatments, especially those that may require new and exciting variations on corporate standards. These people are attentive to the adherence to standards and restrictions. The HR and legal staff are eager to see observance of corporate and legal policy. The IT staff is responsible for the safe and effective administration of network, LMS, and desktop systems. In academic and other organizations, there are also support people who have an interest in instructional projects, but can severely bog down or disorient the development of instruction. It's important to have their support without interference.

Interested colleagues and support staff can be involved later in the process, but delaying their involvement may make them less understanding and supportive later on. It's usually better to keep the invitee list to those who are most likely to be creative problem solvers with respect to the instructional design process. A smaller group tends to be more productive.

When it comes to the Savvy Start team, quantity is a very decisive issue. Too many cooks spoil the stew and too many people in the Savvy Start will spoil the design. While having many people in the room giving their thoughts and ideas seems like the best approach, it isn't. The Savvy Start is a brainstorming and creative session that requires time for everyone to speak, to be heard, to respond to others, and to tell stories. Having too many people in the room limits the participation of each individual, so it is generally best to keep the Savvy Start team to six or seven people if possible.

Savvy Team vs. Project Team vs. Support Team

Not all Savvy Start team members will continue to participate in design work subsequent to the Savvy Start. Executive stakeholders, for example, can share their expectations, preferences, and criteria at the Savvy Start. Once these have been taken into account and reflected in prototypes, executives may wish to perform only in an approval role going forward or they may delegate such responsibilities and not participate further.

Answers to some key questions will be determined in the Savvy Start, enabling the team to be reduced to a smaller, ongoing project team of workers whose work will be supported, reviewed, and approved by others. The goal is to 1) reduce the Savvy Start team to a task-focused *project team* of more doers and few (if any) sideline experts, and 2) establish a designated *support team* for assistance as needed, review, and approval. Many problems arise from not creating these teams, clearly defining their responsibilities, and securing their availability and commitment.

There are mission-critical expectations to consider when forming the support team, articulating how they will operate, and establishing their roles. Below is a helpful list of expectations for each support team member.

- **Expectation #1**: Team members who need to review design and development milestones will need to be available at specific times, which will be designated in the project plan. A commitment to such availability is critical to schedule and budget.
- **Expectation #2:** Some members will need to commit to several hours every week. Although some project weeks are busier than others, support team members will be needed throughout the project.
- **Expectation #3:** Team members will work with people who have different perspectives and roles in the process. From SMEs to recent learners, the team needs to be willing to consider a variety of perspectives openly.
- **Expectation #4:** Everyone needs to be on task. Responsiveness is critical. Lack of responsiveness can cripple the project and compromise the possibility of success.

THE SAVVY START AGENDA

Even though the Savvy Start is a creative brainstorming session, an agenda or a plan of action is important and necessary. Because everyone is encouraged to discuss their ideas, past experiences, and expectations, an agenda is needed to keep the sessions on track.

The Savvy Start usually begins with a review of the process, expectations of outcomes, and examples of good and bad instruction related to the subject matter. The meeting should conclude with a discussion of how the project is going to proceed following the meeting. The middle is filled with creative brainstorming and design (see Figure 7-2).

Figure 7-2. Savvy Start Activities

Review process, expectations, and examples. Iteratively: brainstorm, design, and prototype. Select designs, assign people to teams, and determine next steps.

The sample agenda in Figure 7-3 is a good start, but project leaders should adapt this agenda to meet their particular situation. For example, if the project is having only a two-day meeting, it may not be possible to prototype as many learning events. The group should consider ramifications of agenda adaptations when prioritizing agenda items on the first day.

Useful guidelines for preparing a Savvy Start agenda:

1. Each session begins with a process review.
2. The second and third days begin with a review of the previous day's accomplishments and unfinished tasks.
3. Each day ends with a wrap-up discussion.
4. Breaks are valuable and needed to provide mental restoration and time for prototyping.

Figure 7-3. Sample of a Savvy Start Agenda

SAVVY START

1 hour	**1 — Kickoff** • Introduce attendees. • Discuss prototyping process and review the three-day agenda. • Review examples of effective and ineffective learning programs relevant to the project at hand.
1.5 hours	**2 — Discuss Goals and Constraints** • Discuss the organization's desired performance goals in behavioral terms. • Present the training/learning climate and readiness for learning as understood from backgrounding. • Share what is known about budget and timeline. • Review the criteria for success: How will the learners' success be measured? • Review previous work done, if any. • Listen to a recent learner's story and solicit the supervisor's and SME's input. (This time may include a review/synthesis of existing curricular materials.)

	• Quickly sketch a map of what the instruction should accomplish. • Discuss delivery platform capabilities and restrictions.
1.5 hours	**3 — Brainstorm** • Discuss how to determine what needs to be taught. • Review the goals and select learning events to prototype. What do learners really need to do? • Discuss the necessity of the learner's motivation to learn. What design elements can be used to heighten motivation? • Brainstorm learning events, including what needs to happen before, during, and after them.
Lunch break? 1.5 hours	**4 — Build Prototype** • Instructional designer(s) and prototyper(s) write objectives and prototype related learning events. • Everyone else is free to check email, go back to work, etc. • Summon the team.
Remainder of the day	**5 — Review Prototype and Repeat** • Review the prototype(s). • Discuss strengths and weaknesses. What worked? What didn't? • Repeat 3, 4, and 5 (at least 2 more times), then: Plan next steps. What happens next? Who else gets involved? How will you move forward?
Day 2 1 hour	**6 — User Feedback** • Review prototypes produced overnight. • Discuss importance of user feedback. • Strategize approaches for user testing.

45 minutes	**7 — Organize Objectives** • Review goals; restate if appropriate. • Draft first objectives x treatments matrix with many holes left open. (Review purpose of matrix as needed.) • Discuss who is going to analyze needed behaviors the Savvy Start team won't address and write corresponding objectives. How will consensus be achieved for these additional course objectives?
30–45 minutes	**8 — Determine Appropriate Assessment and Tracking** • Review goals for assessment. • Stipulate the kinds of assessments to be used. • Discuss performance tracking requirements and mechanisms already in place or needed. • Determine compliance and accessibility.

1 hour	**9 — The Right Solution**
	• Describe the most desired solution, given the conversations throughout the previous two days regarding need, analysis, gap, potential solutions, tracking, assessments, etc. Then ask:
	  • What items would it track?
	  • How would you know learners gained knowledge and experience?
	  • What kind of reporting data would it generate?
	  • How would it be accessed, and what type of security would be present?
	  • Discuss who is best prepared to contribute to the ideal solution. Who, for example, can contribute not only content expertise, but also learning and performance inspiration?

Lunch break? 30 minutes	**10 — Media** • Present a variety of applications using different approaches to media. Discuss pros and cons of different styles. • Gather feedback and opinions on what defines the desired look and feel.
30 minutes	**11 — Agree on Process Continuation** • Review the process for creating the complete application (completion of objectives x treatments matrix, integrating prototypes, number of cycles needed, integrating media, and developing the alpha, beta, and gold versions). • Finalize means of gathering user feedback.
1 hour	**12 — Final Strategy Review** • Review project risks. • Discuss what to expect in the project plan. • Discuss any final questions about next steps and the process as a whole.

CUSTOMIZING THE SAVVY START

In the best case, there would be time, resources, and opportunity to implement every aspect of the ideal Savvy Start, but circumstances seldom provide the best case. Many teams struggle to design and create engaging instructional events in the midst of over-filled days and myriad responsibilities. Unfortunately, it is often necessary to compromise. An important thing to remember is that you are not alone in your struggle. Our studios frequently find it challenging to help clients do what they want to do. Just arranging client schedules to carve out enough time to execute a successful Savvy Start can be difficult.

Customizing the Savvy Start needs to be done with care because so much depends on getting a good start. Creative momentum is difficult to create and even more difficult to maintain. If activities must be removed or reduced, planners should make sure to consider the impact and adjust accordingly. They should try to make substitutions and changes that won't compromise the ability of the group to make good decisions. For example, perhaps people could spend some time before the Savvy Start discussing the organization's current training or learning environment. If the team consists of colleagues who already know each other, introductions aren't necessary. Kick-off time can be reduced by beginning with the discussion of the learning goals for the project.

It's always important to conduct a quick review of SAM, especially the Savvy Start, the organization's desired performance goals, and examples of excellent relevant instructional models at the start of the meeting to ensure everyone is prepared and ready to be creative.

PREPARING THE ROOM

Having the right tools and resources in the Savvy Start is essential to facilitate discussions effectively and to document the meeting properly. Below is a list of items you will probably need in the room:

- flip charts (we find that the ones with adhesive backing are the best)
- markers
- tape or push pins (in case the flip charts aren't adhesive)
- a dry erase board (this can be in lieu of or in addition to the flip charts)
- dry erase markers (don't mix these up with the permanent ones!)
- water, mints, nuts, fruit, cheese, soda, coffee, and tea (it's best to keep people in the room).

Optional (required if e-learning is to be part of the solution) but very handy:

- computer(s) (for reviewing samples and for the prototyper)
- Internet connection
- a video projector.

Additionally, the Savvy Start team will need the collected background information and resources. Appropriate documents should be prepared for distribution if this was not done before the Savvy Start.

CONDUCTING THE SAVVY START

The Savvy Start sets the tone for the entire project. It's a unique type of meeting that combines creative evaluation, brainstorming, storytelling, prototyping, planning, and revision. Through this creative process, you and your team will build the foundation for subsequent iterations that will shape what the instructional product will become.

The Savvy Start succeeds in an environment that encourages creativity and productivity. It needs to be focused on completing tasks rather than just having everyone speak. Although all should be encouraged to participate, not everyone should offer an opinion on every subject.

Since it's likely that participants may never have experienced the process before, time needs to be set aside for:

- laying out the ground rules and setting performance goals
- discussing previous learning experiences the target audience has had
- explaining successive approximation
- discussing learning goals in terms of behavior change
- creating a strategic map.

It is best to strive for two or three full days to accommodate all of the activities necessary for a successful Savvy Start. Shortened Savvy Starts are seldom satisfactory, but how much time is needed depends on many factors, such as the volume of content and whether tasks to be learned are of a similar nature or highly divergent. It also depends on whether the organization is upgrading existing curriculum or setting out anew.

Due to the number of variables, perhaps no two Savvy Starts should ever be alike. In any case, it's unlikely they have been. It's important for the leader and the team to own the process and feel comfortable with it. But it has nuances to it, some counterintuitive, perhaps. Probably the more counterintuitive they are, the more important it is to do them in the right way. The notes that follow may be helpful for conducting selected activities in the process.

Kick-Off

The way meetings start influences what follows. The Savvy Start is no different. The meeting needs to begin with a friendly, collaborative tone because spirited differences of opinion are likely to emerge fairly soon. It should also be made clear this meeting is not going to be the typical old-style meeting to which everyone is accustomed. There are many ways to accomplish that: Give everyone a brightly colored hat or place card with a label of something the individual might be responsible for to ensure the meeting is both fun and productive. Consider: "Fair," "On Schedule," "Creative," "Practical," "Open," "Considerate," and so on.

Does everyone know each other and what they do in the organization? Even if they do, people probably have different hopes for the project. It's good practice to ask everyone to share his or her hopes and expectations right away.

To break the ice, the leader might say, "Everyone's opinion is vital to our success. If someone else could provide the input you are uniquely qualified to offer, you wouldn't be here. As we go around the room, please describe your role and give us a brief description of your favorite learning events. That will help us all better understand your hopes and concerns for this project!"

The Agenda

The leader should take a moment to review the agenda, explain the process, and ensure the team understands the schedule. Depending on the savvy experience of the group, this step may not take very long at all.

Assuming there has been a careful selection of attendees, everyone's whole-hearted participation is a must for this project to be a success. The leader should be well prepared to

- crisply present the target outcomes for the Savvy Start
- establish ground rules for how the group will work together
- get everyone involved early in the meeting
- review the stages and phases of the development process.

The importance of a knowledgeable, skilled, confident, and enthusiastic leader cannot be overstated. Getting specific, following is an outline of what the leader does.

Ground Rules

The Savvy Start leader will need to set some ground rules to ensure a collaborative, creative, and productive meeting. From keeping track of time, to moving through the agenda, to controlling dominant talkers and subordinate thinkers, a clear set of rules helps everyone. Some good rules to share are:

1. Be responsible for contributing constructive ideas and opinions.
2. If you don't wish to speak, no one will call on you. (Not everyone needs to share an opinion on everything.)
3. If you have not shared a contrary point of view, silence indicates concurrence. It will not be constructive to raise surprise objections later.
4. Keep comments as brief as possible.
5. The schedule keeper has the right to limit discussion if necessary to manage time and productivity.
6. Turn mobile phones off and put them out of sight.
7. It's OK to change your mind and helpful if you share your new perspective.

This is the beginning of a creative process, and it is important that everyone in the room feels safe and comfortable discussing ideas and opinions.

Successive Approximation Method (SAM)

SAM, which is shared in detail throughout this book, may not be a process with which all or any attendees are familiar. Perhaps the most fundamental principle is that work progresses in small steps to allow for frequent course corrections and to avoid spending too much resource on one component. Early ideas and prototypes are not expected to endure, but rather be replaced by the better ideas and designs they engender. Throwing out early ideas is a step of progress, not failure. People representative of the targeted learners need to share their reactions even during the design phases, as only they can see things through their eyes. All process participants must understand these and the other principles of SAM.

Some principles of SAM probably run counter to thoughts and preferences of some group members. We've found SAM can be difficult to comprehend until having experienced it once. Observing or participating in SAM is essential to appreciating what SAM is and how effective it is. We've never heard of anyone wanting to abandon it after giving SAM an earnest try, but it can take some nudging to hazard that first try. Clarity about SAM is important here so people understand what they are going try.

In addition to the items on the agenda, people may wonder how they can be sure they are creating great learning. They may be concerned about their role and perhaps that of others. The team needs to understand that the iterative process itself will enable them to:
- ensure the design stays on track with budget and schedule
- allow more experimentation and evaluation
- garner the most in-process feedback from the team and the organization
- create meaningful, memorable, and motivational learning experiences
- develop the best possible product with given resources.

SAM has three phases, eight stages, and seven different tasks. It may look like a lot, but most of the process makes intuitive sense and is repetitive. It's the iterations that may be a foreign construct that takes a little getting used to. Luckily, not all members of the Savvy Start will be involved in tasks undertaken in later phases, so not a lot of detail need be covered now.

Figure 7-4. An Overview of SAM

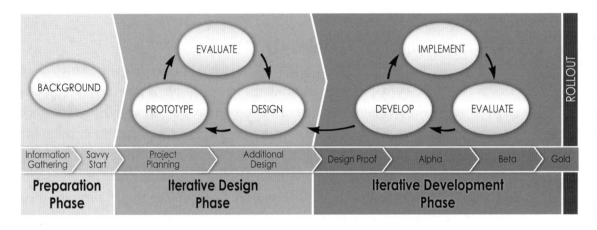

Referring to the diagram in Figure 7-4, it is enough to explain to the team that prior to the Savvy Start:

- Information was collected regarding the rationale for the project.
- Existing content was gathered (if it was).
- Initial success parameters were drafted for the group's approval.

Referring back to the successive approximation chapter as necessary, the leader should be able to describe the process effectively and answer any questions about it.

Learning Goals

Stating the learning goal proposed for the project and keeping it in mind is essential to maintaining focus and direction for the group's work throughout the Savvy Start and the whole project. Reviewing the goal may seem redundant to what was learned and accomplished during backgrounding, but what was identified then may have been heavily biased by the source of the information or by invalid assumptions. The people in the room may have a broader and more helpful view of what the goals should be or even a completely different set of goals in mind.

Once set, the selected goal must not be forgotten as focus turns to the many issues ahead. All too often projects wander off track because the goal was not really agreed to, not clearly defined, or not reiterated often enough. While in the throes of creative brainstorming, it becomes easy to lose sight of what's important and where you intended to go.

Although teams should be open to course correction and seizing greater opportunities than were first evident, the team should continually validate decisions against the selected goal to avoid getting caught up in the "what *can* be done" seduction versus the "what *should* be done" mission. This conflict arises when undirected creativity overrides sound, goal-oriented judgment. The learning goals and criteria for success of the project must be used to curtail fruitless excursions and embellishments that provide little or no benefit.

Goal-Oriented Design vs. SAM

Despite all the comments and recommendations in the preceding discussion, balance is needed with respect to sticking to the goal and the process of successive approximation. A source of pride is not that the team stuck to the original goal if, through iterative brainstorming and prototyping, the team recognized the goal wasn't actually what it should be and could be. Even the goal needs to be subject to iterative reconsideration. Blindly sticking to the original goal when it falls into question subverts the iterative process into a more linear one—exactly what SAM is intended to supplant.

At the same time, SAM does not succeed if the team vacillates on everything, including the primary project goal. Therefore, while goal re-evaluation is appropriate during the Savvy Start, the goal should be stated and agreed upon before moving to the next phase of iterative design. It's smart to post it on the wall as a constant reminder.

The Organization's Training Environment

Within every organization are unrecognized challenges to successfully implementing instructional initiatives. Examining the training environment as a whole is essential to ensure the project will have the greatest impact possible. Challenges and hurdles within the organization that may limit the effectiveness of performance improvement efforts should be identified before design and development have been completed.

Consider such factors as:
- Do the learners value learning? Is it in their best interest to perform better?
- What have learners responded well to in the past?
- Have previous instructional programs been considered boring time-wasters? What made them so?
- Do learners have access to media-capable computers and know how to use them?
- Are learners located where they can concentrate and work with sufficient privacy and focus?
- Are knowledgeable instructors available? Or will someone be "teaching the book"?
- Is there adequate bandwidth and IT support? Are firewalls going to prevent use of needed communications and technology?

Although the organization's climate may not be perfect, there should be hope that existing problems can be overcome. Discussing known issues will help rule out certain solutions that would pose too many challenges or require too many organizational adjustments.

Previous Work

Current training is worth reviewing even if it's on different topics. You won't want to repeat an approach or strategy that doesn't work well in the organization, and you'll certainly want to take advantage of those that do.

Background information may provide a basis to discuss past experiences with the group. The team will undoubtedly want to share techniques they have used, what the outcomes were, and what lessons they learned from their experiences. This is a time to gather more information about past efforts to improve performance, and perhaps reveal a bit more about the learning climate than anyone was cognizant of. This discussion shouldn't be limited to just the instruction, but should also include the strategies used to support behavior changes—incentives, mentors, field trips, job aids, and so on.

Stories Set the Stage

The review of the previous work probably elicited a lot of stories from the group. Storytelling is a great way to communicate the details of a situation or event that may not otherwise be considered. Urging the group to tell their stories will add volumes of important and relevant information.

Recent learners, teachers, and job supervisors can also share helpful and insightful stories about past learning experiences and the changes that followed or didn't. Hopefully there are recent learners in the Savvy Start group. Since recent learner insights are exceptionally beneficial, the team should strive to make them comfortable enough speak up.

Some questions for recent learners:
- What was easy to learn?
- What was difficult?
- Why was it difficult and what helped?
- How did you "get" it?
- What did you find fascinating, if anything?
- Was anything boring and if so, why was it boring to you?
- What was useful and what was unnecessary?

- What are you doing differently on the job because of what you learned?
- What was unnecessary to cover in your learning program?
- What valuable tips have you learned from colleagues?

Since instructors and supervisors observe the successes and failures of people similar to your project's learners, their stories can be useful to understanding what is worthwhile and what isn't, what is consequential and unimportant, and what is needed and what is not.

Success Defined

What do we think is good instruction or learning? Not all participants are likely to be learning experts, but strong opinions may well exist anyway. Divergent opinions need to surface, and yet the instructional designer needs to guide the group to agreement. Liking or disliking something that happened to an individual as a learner isn't a good basis for design, but it may well suggest an appropriate acceptance criterion. The key here is to get acceptance criteria stated explicitly and then agreed to. If not everyone agrees, then practicality dictates the key decision maker should state what he or she requires.

Many instructional projects have, whether stated or not, the same unfortunate criteria for success. Was it completed on time? Was it within the budget? Did it cover all of the content? Did it open with a list of learning objectives and conclude with a test? Did it roll out smoothly? Were there few learner complaints? But these measures of success are relevant only to the project and not to the performance outcomes achieved, which are, theoretically at least, the primary goal of the project.

Whether it's improved math skills, leadership, customer service, sales, time-to-market, or reduced errors or recalls, there is a need to establish how the impact of instruction on developing needed abilities and changing behaviors will be measured. The criteria for success should effectively identify whether the instruction addressed the discrepancy between what is now occurring and what should be occurring.

Each desired behavior may have numerous measures of success, so it may not be possible to identify them all. However, it is important to establish what will be measured before designing the treatments to accomplish the stated goal.

Performance Goals

Most projects are created to improve the performance of individuals and the organization they're a part of by developing effective skills and behaviors. The learning experiences being developed will serve as the means for this change. In some cases the goal is to teach skills learners don't have, such as speaking French or Japanese. In other cases, current behaviors are ineffective and need to be replaced by more effective behaviors.

In the latter case, it's helpful to begin by identifying the current behaviors, the problems these behaviors cause, the correct behaviors, and what can be achieved through instruction. There can be a gap between what the learner can do and does do, i.e. a *performance gap*; or a gap between what the learner can do and needs to be able to do, i.e. a *skill gap*. If learners can already perform as needed, instructional solutions are likely to have little effect. If learners lack the ability to perform, then instruction is an appropriate component of the solution. Obviously, it's important to know which type of gap you have before designing a solution.

Many teams start by creating two columns on a flip chart or whiteboard. They title the first column "Current Behaviors" and the second column "Desired Behaviors." Then, keeping the project's overall goal in mind, they brainstorm some goals. For example:

Current Behaviors	Desired Behaviors	Goals
Factory workers release automobiles with misaligned doors	Factory workers verify door fit and correct misalignments immediately after attachment	Factory workers verify fit, finish, and function immediately after attachment of parts
Instructional designers are using post-tests to motivate learning	Instructional designers avoid motivation of short-term learning behavior	Instructional designers use intrigue and engagement to motivate in-depth learning

They discuss what problem behaviors, if any, contribute to this issue. It's important to stay on track by focusing on behaviors needed to achieve the overall goal. There may be many skills missing and many problem behaviors not directly associated with the goal at hand that should be tabled for another discussion.

Once the group has identified all of the skills needed and problem behaviors to be eradicated, if any, they can work to identify probable causes for the problem behaviors and list behaviors for each of the skill gaps identified. By posting these behavior lists in a prominent place in the room, they can be used throughout the meeting as a way to keep the discussion focused on closing the skill or performance gap.

Skills Hierarchy

Before moving on to designing learning events, the performance goals and associated tasks should be organized into a map or skills hierarchy. The hierarchy identifies all the skills performers need and connects more complex skills (or behaviors) with simpler, less complex skills. It quickly and easily contributes to an understanding of the magnitude of the proposed project and often suggests a reduction from original aspirations.

Design tip: The temptation to begin teaching at the bottom of the hierarchy and work up should be avoided, as that's a recipe for kicking off instruction with the least interesting content.

A skills hierarchy is easy to construct. Participants write a desired behavior, one the project is to help develop, on a sticky note or card and stick or tape it high on a wall or whiteboard. Then, working downward, participants post prerequisite skills required to perform behaviors above them. They continue adding skills until they reach a base level of skills the target population is sure to have (see Figure 7-5).

Figure 7-5. Skills Hierarchy Chart Example

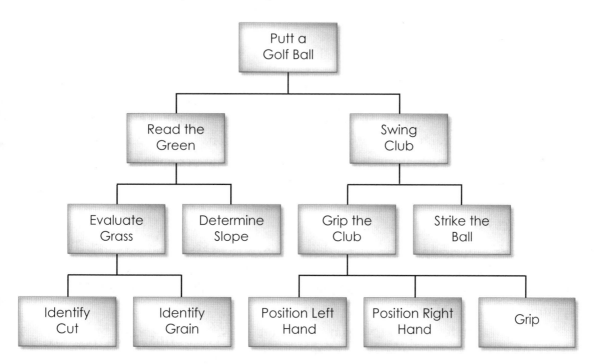

Through discussions that add, move, and remove skills, the team can narrow in on what skills must be taught. Skills that enable more than one higher order skill can be grouped into clusters for modularity and more work space.

PROTOTYPING AND EVALUATION

The Savvy Start is the first use of the iterative process of evaluation, design, and development in SAM. Iterations are done very quickly with sketches and prototypes that represent possible design directions. The primary difference between the Savvy Start and the iterative design phase is the participants. The design iterations to follow are usually done by a smaller work group. Their work is then reviewed and approved by members selected from the Savvy Start team.

The Savvy Start serves somewhat different purposes from the iterative design phase, however. While we expect the Savvy Start to generate some useful prototypes, it is more importantly a way of determining answers to these critical success questions:

- How will decisions be made and by whom?
- Who is really in charge—the ultimate decision maker (if there is one)?
- What is it going to cost to do what we think we should do?
- How rigid are the given constraints?
- How accurate is the gathered background information?
- What should be reanalyzed?
- What additional information is needed?
- Do we have the right team?

Answers to these questions are difficult to find at first glance, but the Savvy Start event is quite effective in revealing them. Without this information, which is not typically elicited through other ISD models, projects are vulnerable to countless crippling hazards. It's crucial to know this information before entering the iterative design phase.

Savvy Start II

It's not all that unusual to need to regroup and conduct a second Savvy Start. Too much information may have been lacking. The wrong people, too many, or too few may have participated. It may be recognized that the project as originally envisioned would not be an appropriate solution after all.

Needing to abandon ship or try again should not be viewed as failure. Quite the contrary, the ability of the Savvy Start to generate reconsiderations quickly and efficiently is a primary advantage of the

It's not unusual to need to regroup and conduct a second Savvy Start.

process. Getting started on the right foot, headed in the right direction, and identifying the right path to meet the specific needs of an organization is critical to the success of any process. The Savvy Start is invaluable for this as it brings unique sensitivity and responsiveness to the project. If SAM did nothing more than produce the benefits of the Savvy Start, it would be a major advantage over traditional processes that are insensitive to the unique circumstances surrounding projects.

WRAP UP

The creative SAM process needs a team that understands and supports its values and principles. As with many processes, a successful start brings great rewards.

The Savvy Start is an effective way of addressing critical questions—questions that are often asked far before they can be answered credibly: *How much will it cost to provide a successful learning solution for our performance needs? What resources are required? How long will it take?* These questions are often asked naively, but in earnest. Without having the information the Savvy Start provides, the questions cannot be answered accurately. It's a bit like asking how much it would cost to build a new house without knowing anything about the lot it would be placed on, the style of the house, the number of bedrooms and baths, and so on.

Addressing what is going to happen next, soliciting the team's ongoing support, and reviewing the discoveries and recommendations from the Savvy Start will prepare the organization well for the following phases and into delivery of successful learning.

Prototyping in the Savvy Start and iterative design is critical to the whole SAM approach. It's such a critical component that it gets a full chapter, which follows next.

CHAPTER 8

Prototyping

Prototypes are an invaluable, core component of the SAM process. They provide an indispensable means of sharing information among key stakeholders and lead to more creative designs. Prototypes are indispensable because no other means provides as much clarity to the proposed design and assures alignment of expectations. If some team members believe they have agreed to design decisions that are different from what others thought they agreed to, project-crippling trouble lies ahead, especially if the difference is discovered after the product is developed. Even slight ambiguities at the beginning can cause serious problems in the final product.

SKETCHING

There are many types of prototypes—such as content scoping and page layout—and ways of conveying design ideas, such as sketching, outlining, and wire framing. Sketching has terrific advantages as a start to any creative process, and is especially valuable in an iterative one where speed and minimal expense are critical. Bill Buxton, in his seminal book on sketching user interface designs (2007), points out the superior benefits of sketches for collaboration and creative brainstorming. Not only are sketches fast and inexpensive, they invite others to contribute ideas in supportive ways. Their informality says *I've got an idea that I'm kicking around and I wonder if you can help me,* and sidesteps what might otherwise make responses feel like criticisms.

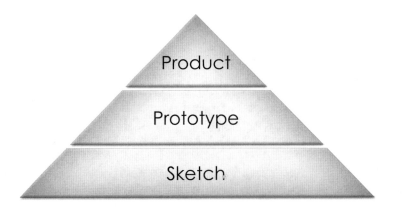

Buxton differentiates sketches from prototypes. Prototypes take more effort, have greater refinement, have more functionality, and serve more to test the feasibility of an idea than to generate ideas. Raising concerns about a prototype more easily generates rebuttals and defensiveness, whereas concerns about a sketch can seem more collaborative.

WHY BUILD PROTOTYPES

While sketches are invaluable for generating ideas and getting everyone on the same track, it's not wise to skip from sketches to product production or even product planning. This is especially true with technology or media-enhanced learning; there are too many unanswered design questions for the mechanics involved.

With e-learning, timing, transitions, and media interleave to create experiences. Words can't adequately describe a media-rich interaction. Functional prototypes are indispensable because e-learning interactivity needs to be witnessed and experienced for evaluation. Even the most experienced interactivity designers are regularly surprised by a design that worked well in their minds, but came up short when prototyped. Conversely, having the prototype to work with can not only point out deficiencies, but also reveal unseen opportunities that would not be apparent in sketches or specification documents.

Looking at sketches only, people may easily form incorrect assumptions about what others are thinking and intending to do. If incorrect assumptions are made about what was intended, the final product will depart significantly from expectations and may prove to be totally unacceptable to reviewers and stakeholders.

An example of each design progression step is demonstrated in the following graphics. (See Figures 8-1 to 8-3.)

Figure 8-1. Design Sketch

Initial sketches need to be done quickly, not only to fit the schedule but also to invite conversation, modification, and for most sketches, abandonment. Sketches get messy with modifications, but this is good because at some point, it becomes obviously necessary to start over. Starting over, perhaps many times, gives rise to new thoughts and makes it easy to abandon those that shouldn't carry forward. Each time you redraw a sketch, you also think about what is really worth keeping.

Figure 8-2. Design Prototype

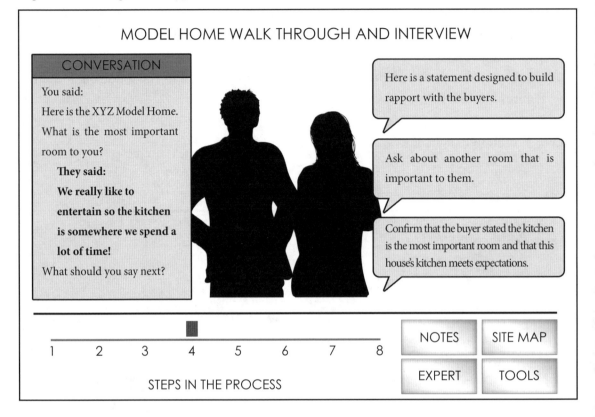

Promising sketches move forward to prototypes. Again, speed is a primary target because multiple prototypes are better than one. Even here in prototypes, "blah, blah, blah" text is often more appropriate than any thoughtful wording. Functionality should be built only for key components of the instructional interactivity. Other screen objects should be left as dummies or placeholders to support some thought about screen layout and future functionality.

Figure 8-3. Final Product

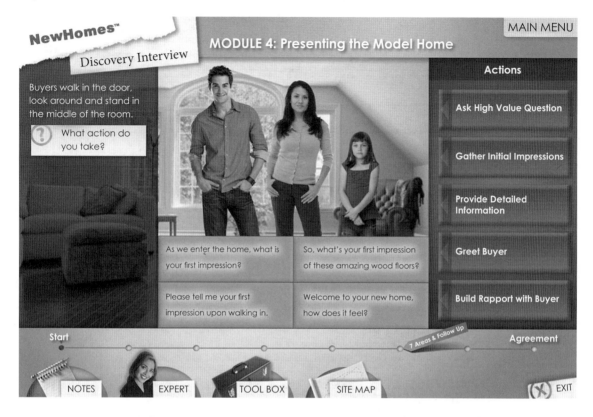

In development, the product gets refined screen layout, polished graphics, and full functionality. The relationship to prototypes is clear, but it's also likely that many elements have been improved.

e-Sketches

The difference between sketches and prototypes actually blurs a bit with the increasing ease and rapidity that some new tools have brought to prototyping. Balsamiq Mockups (balsamiq.com), for example, makes electronic sketching of screen design ideas very easy and quick (see Figure 8-4 on the next page).

Figure 8-4. Design Sketch Using Balsamiq

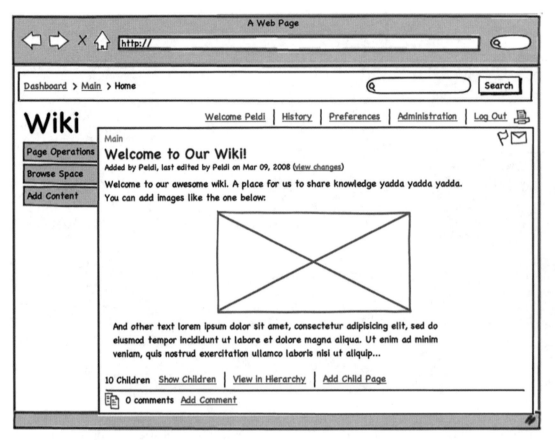

Figure courtesy of Balsamiq Studios, LLC.

The product falls somewhere between the truly informal, "I'm just thinking about this" napkin sketch and an idea presentation. The clever, imprecise style representing pencil drawings softens the edge that might otherwise make these enhanced sketches work more as a pitch than a discussion. Collaboration software and cloud technology allow multiple authors to comment online and create derivations for team review.

Going the next step, ZebraZapps (zebrazapps.com) (see Figure 8-5) makes sketches functional with very little effort and time, so reviewers can appraise essential notions of interactivity that evolve into rich-media events.

Figure 8-5. Functional Design Sketch Using ZebraZapps

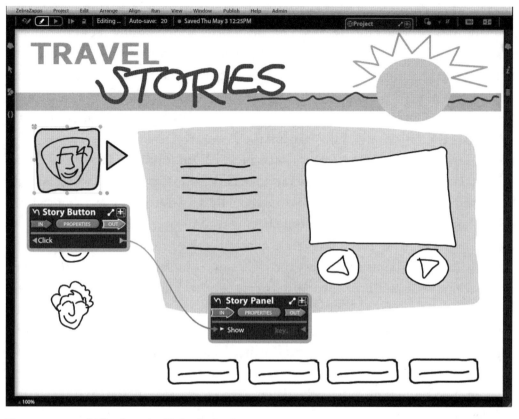

Figure courtesy of Allen Learning Technologies, Inc.

The challenge is to preserve the informality and genial nature of sketches while being sufficiently precise about intended interactivity and use of media. To achieve the former, the style needs to suggest the sketch was made very quickly. While a polished look can be achieved with remarkable speed using today's software tools for drawing and illustration, visual refinement subverts the power of sketches and is to be avoided. This is an important notion so well captured by the developers at Balsamiq. Not only must sketches be rough, but they must also give the impression that a small amount of time was invested in them and imply the sketcher is open to alternative ideas.

ZebraZapps allows sketchers to make their sketches functional. A quickly drawn button, for example, can be made to actually work and present a roughly sketched illustration, video drawn from YouTube, travel location, smile or frown, or anything. Quickly produced, rough prototypes are inexpensive and disposable. Most importantly, they can function as sketches in that no one hesitates to put forth modifications and no one feels compelled to defend an initial design because of the effort invested.

Extra Benefits of Prototypes

The bonus of building prototypes is that by finding problems and opportunities early, before development begins, overall process time can be shorted dramatically. Fewer changes, corrections, and iterations in the higher cost development phase mean lower total costs and less total project time. Getting a product out faster is so important to many organizations that this one benefit alone is enough to demand the use of prototyping. But it is the ability of prototypes to help people be more creative, talk more constructively about design, and develop the same expectations that fully warrant their use.

To better understand the importance of prototyping, consider times you may have seen the movie of a book you have read. Were characters, places, and events just as you imagined them? Of course, movie directors sometimes intentionally depart from the text, but viewers and directors often see different images despite having read the same verbal description.

Prototyping in SAM is more than just an effort to create an interaction or course module quickly. It's a collaborative process that serves to complete the critical analysis of what learners really need and how those needs can be met. The process of prototyping, reviewing, and prototyping again clarifies the team's emerging insights and hones everyone's expectations for what events, situations, activities, topics, and information learners will need. The prototype is a synthesis of content, instructional approach, values, expectations, and, of course, technology.

Brainstorming and discussing design ideas allows many ideas to emerge from the design process, while the controlled iterative process keeps things moving forward. Ideas that sounded great at first, at least to the contributor, will be revised as the team seeks to answer the questions, "What if the learning experiences could…," "Wouldn't it be better if…," and "What should learners really do?" Reviewing ideas not just verbally, but also in sketches and then in prototype form sparks more ideas and demonstrates why some ideas are not fitting into the emerging design.

Although a prototype is the first attempt to create the final instructional treatment, a prototype should not be thought of as a draft. Rather, the quick prototype is a method for examining more closely the design options of serious interest to the team. First attempts can be reviewed and revised to iterate toward the final interaction, or simply discarded if they are deemed ineffective.

Stuart Pugh's insights into concept generation and selection (as cited in Buxton, 2007), describe the process as it usually goes in successive approximation (see Figure 8-6). A large number of ideas come from preconceptions and initial brainstorming. As ideas are evaluated, some are discarded while others are combined to merge toward a selection. But as synthesis occurs and some possibilities are eliminated, new ideas arrive to drive the number of considerations back up a bit. As the new ideas are evaluated in the overall emerging approach, some again will be discarded and others combined. Thus, the number of ideas shrinks only to generate a few fresh ideas. Through iterative expansion and reduction of ideas, a carefully considered selection survives.

Figure 8-6. Concept Generation and Selection

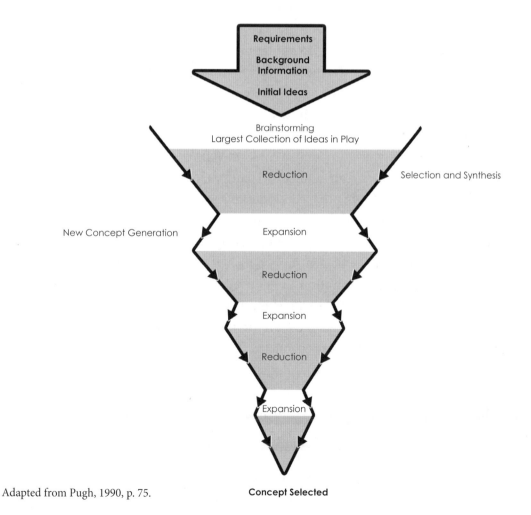

Adapted from Pugh, 1990, p. 75.

Interim prototypes help in the process of both discarding and discovering design ideas. The number of ideas expands and contracts until ultimately, the process culminates in one or a few prototyped ideas worthy of development.

THE ESSENCE OF A PROTOTYPE

So what exactly is a prototype? A prototype is a tangible embodiment of an idea or concept. It can be an outline of class session activities. It can be instructor notes. It can be instructions to learners for performing a learning exercise.

A prototype is, by definition, rough and incomplete. A prototype is *not* a fully functioning instructional component with presentable images, thoughtful narratives, and complete content. It is *not* a typo-free instructor guide or formatted learner guide.

A prototype uses stick figures, squares, and circles in place of polished media. In e-learning, a prototype is a roughly constructed interactive component that has few words and either no media or just handy stand-in media or sketches. An e-learning prototype only has the level of functionality necessary to witness key, proposed interactivity and discuss its desirability. Prototypes provide the means to click, drag, highlight, select, or sequence in order to demonstrate the interactivity of the design. While more interactivity is valuable, it needs to be limited to prevent so much investment in an idea that it seems wasteful to discard the work, even if it doesn't seem fitting when evaluated. Early prototypes often demonstrate only one activity or exercise in a multi-step interaction.

Interactive components devoid of refined art and well-written prose allow people to clearly see what would happen with prospective designs while wasting little time developing an idea that may be discarded. Simple—albeit ugly—screens are the best way to clearly expose the design and keep team members contributing.

In addition to wasting valuable design time, polished art (or even refined interactivity) too often garners misguided admiration and obscures weaknesses in the design. This admiration may cause the team to feel that it shouldn't abandon such a wonderful creation, when in reality the design may be inadequate or ineffective. The challenge of effective prototyping is to keep the team focused on the functionality instead of how it looks. Keeping the prototypes simple, colorless, and unembellished can limit the risk of tending to concerns that should be taken up later.

Nonetheless (and predictably), some team members will have trouble distinguishing between critical design elements and superficial components such as colors, layout, graphic style, wording, and so on. These individuals usually do not have a well-developed sensitivity for instructional design and need a more refined visualization to appreciate it. While participating in the process a few times may help them better appreciate the role of early, imperfect prototypes, it is often helpful to have examples of completed projects that demonstrate various levels and types of polish, look, and feel that can facilitate brief discussions concerning those issues. Rapid prototyping is essential, but it's also important to satisfy concerns that otherwise prevent team members from focusing on key issues.

Media, colors, wording, and interactivity refinements can distract the team from the core design issues. Once the topics are on the table, they can command endless amounts of discussion time. It's important not to be derailed into developing prototypes that address refinement issues or spending significant amounts of time on such topics to the detriment of addressing fundamentals. Building special-purpose prototypes at this point in the process will result in both continuing requests for more, as well as diversion from higher level issues. Speed is the measure of success with prototypes, and moving forward matters. So use existing examples rather than creating new ones.

Figure 8-7. Initial Prototype—Medical Context

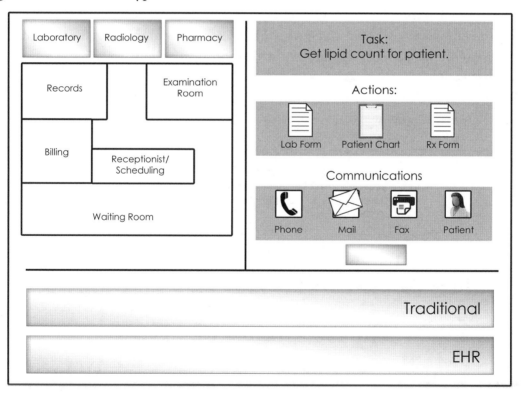

E-LEARNING PROTOTYPES

For e-learning, initial prototypes are essentially sketches with moving parts for defining, considering, and evaluating a learning experience. Some text, buttons, dragable objects, interactions, and feedback are often enough.

The example on the previous page (Figure 8-7) used the context of a medical clinic. The learner is presented with the task of getting a lipid count. Proper procedures will be needed to communicate with and manage the patient, obtain a blood test, fill out forms, and so on. The learner has several options for completing the task and can access both traditional health records and electronic health records as the clinic converts to new processes. This prototype helped the design team decide what was essential to making the context authentic and what would make interactions overly complex.

A blend of sketching and prototyping is possible with some tools as shown in the example on the next page (Figure 8-8) done in ZebraZapps. Here the informality of the sketching most strongly encourages team members to focus on content and propose alternatives. Because this tool allows elements of sketches to take on as much functionality as is helpful and do so very quickly without changing from sketches to computer-generated graphics (unless desired), the team can explore alternatives of functionality, pedagogy, and content quickly and as one.

Figure 8-8. Initial Prototype—IT Content

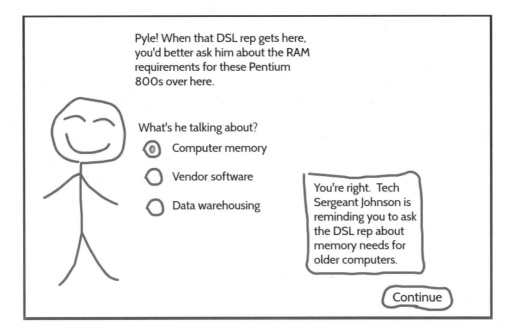

Prototypes go through a series of modifications and replacements as the team searches for the right designs. Figure 8-9 traces prototyping activities from Savvy Start to design proof, indicating how prototypes serve different functions at different points in the process. Early prototypes must be visually crude and unrefined to support brainstorming. They are intended to be disposable. Later prototypes become more detailed and refined to convey aesthetic standards, integration of media, expected reading level, and so on. These prototypes can evolve into the final product.

Figure 8-9. Life Cycle of a Prototype

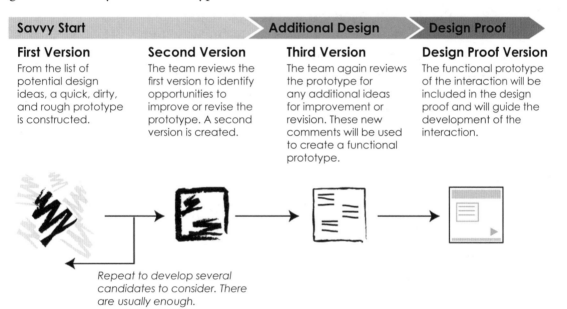

Savvy Start		Additional Design	Design Proof
First Version	**Second Version**	**Third Version**	**Design Proof Version**
From the list of potential design ideas, a quick, dirty, and rough prototype is constructed.	The team reviews the first version to identify opportunities to improve or revise the prototype. A second version is created.	The team again reviews the prototype for any additional ideas for improvement or revision. These new comments will be used to create a functional prototype.	The functional prototype of the interaction will be included in the design proof and will guide the development of the interaction.

Repeat to develop several candidates to consider. There are usually enough.

The graphics on the next pages (Figures 8-10 to 8-13) show a succession of prototypes. Notice that early prototypes are rough and imprecise as compared to subsequent, more functional prototypes used in the design proof (we'll discuss the design proof more later). Early prototypes are discussion tools for the brainstorming team, instead of a design specification for the final application. Prototypes the team selects will be revised, fine-tuned, and used in the development of the final application.

Figure 8-10. First Version

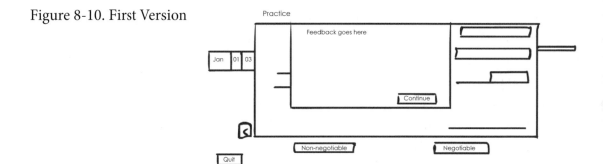

This was the first prototype for a bank teller course in loss prevention—to cover topics such as negotiability, entitlement, authentication, illegal manipulation, etc. The design imagined this treatment where the learner is placed into a rich bank environment with a queue of customers (each representing a different issue and challenge), a simulated work station, cash drawers, telephone lifelines, and colleague conversations. In other words, everything encountered in the real environment. Learner task: successfully resolve the loss-prevention risk associated with each customer interaction.

Figure 8-11. Second Version

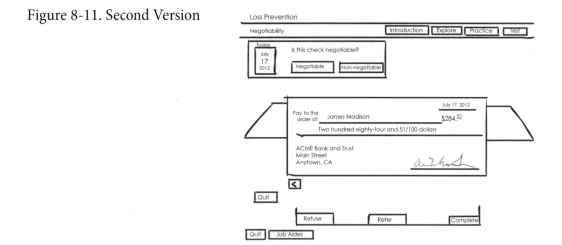

Feedback from evaluation of the first prototype made it clear that the complexity of the simulation was overpowering the basic task of examining the monetary instruments and making decisions. In this second approach, the design focused entirely on the composition of the checks and eliminated much of the manipulation of the physical environment. The idea of a single comprehensive unit is discarded for a modular approach where topics are introduced and practiced individually in short 5-10 minute modules and then only combined in a final "putting it all together" activity.

Figure 8-12. Third Version

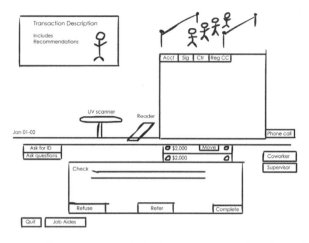

The positive response to the second prototype led the team to develop that design further. Simple contextual elements (the teller station as a background, dynamic calendar, photorealistic checks) were added to the simple design. An overall lesson structure was suggested by the navigation buttons, and the interaction was focused to foster a ritualized approach to establish negotiability was added, where the learner judges the negotiability and then must justify that answer by indicating the lacking elements.

Figure 8-13. Design Proof

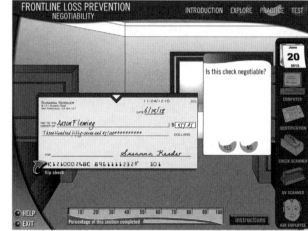

The design proof specifies the full-functioning interaction. The contextual background graphics placing this at the teller station are integrated, the screen layout is set to define sizes of the check graphics and size limitations for blocks of instructions and feedback text, the menu structure is established to define user control of access, and all remaining lesson options and components are accounted for. The design proof encapsulates all the findings of the prototypes for the purpose of validating the design for completeness and providing a clear foundation for subsequent efficient development.

THREE PROTOTYPES, PLUS OR MINUS ONE

Most importantly, prototypes are and must be recognized as disposable. It's important to minimize the effort invested in a prototype, because the greater the investment, the more necessary it will be to continue with the design it represents and bypass exploration of alternatives that might prove superior. The rule is to keep prototypes simple, quick, and imperfect to avoid becoming attached to them.

In my work, I find it useful to make a pact with myself and others at the outset: *No matter how much we like our first prototype, we will develop three—maybe more, but probably three and only three.* Further, I like to restrict myself: *In the second prototype, I will not reuse ideas incorporated in the first. I will try for something completely different.*

As we start out to create a second design and abandon the first, we nearly always feel we can't do it without components from the first design. However, as we resist temptations and stick to the plan, it also almost always occurs that we discover something better.

In the third iteration, while I try again to force myself to invent something new and better, I allow borrowing from the first and second prototypes if it seems absolutely necessary. Whether I borrow or not, the third prototype is usually a keeper. Not always, however. Sometimes we feel we have proven that the first design was, indeed, the best. Sometimes it's clear I need to try once again. But having done at least three, whatever the selection, I have confidence that we have a good design and a far better one than if I had experimented with only one idea.

CHAPTER 9

Constructing the Prototype

Now that we've explored the essence of a prototype and why we build it, we will discuss the essential steps involved in constructing a prototype.

THE HELPFUL PROTOTYPER

A good prototyper is a uniquely talented individual who wields not only the essential technical skills to build functional prototypes quickly, but also the ability to listen carefully to discussions, synthesize information, and formulate designs that embody the strength of the group's combined ideas. If not a skilled instructional designer, the prototyper must be able to partner effectively with a designer to incorporate sound instructional principles.

A good prototyper:
- works quickly and strategically
- reflects ideas of the group
- demonstrates what works and reveals possible problems
- avoids temptation to embellish more than necessary
- listens carefully and thinks of ways to meet multiple criteria
- eagerly explores and demonstrates alternative approaches
- appreciates good instructional design and good graphic design
- discards his or her work with little hesitation.

While this list of requirements is more than challenging, it also includes something of a perverse twist. If the prototyper is a skilled programmer, there will be the additional challenge of abandoning some habits and constructs that are important in developing good software. The careful structuring of code, purposeful naming of variables, and systematic organization of data are unnecessary and even unwelcome where they delay the presentation of a prototype.

Talented prototypers are good at faking things and cheating on development strategies in an effort to build quickly. They are fast, sloppy in some ways, and able to turn imprecise descriptions into prototypes that appear more functional than they actually are. In order to explore as many ideas as possible, these individuals construct prototypes with the least amount of effort possible. They are always on the lookout for shortcuts that save time and effort—shortcuts that would be shunned in their role as a professional courseware developer or programmer.

Because many highly proficient developers cannot abandon their professional scruples, even if they're willing to try, teams shouldn't automatically request their best developers to prototype. It seems sensible to select a talented developer to build prototypes, but others may actually be better suited to the role. Sometimes a limited level of software proficiency is an asset to be preferred over software engineering strengths. Although many talented developers can be outstanding prototypers, this role is much more about speed than perfection. Consider as well junior developers, media artists, or others who possess rudimentary development skills but can cleverly implement ideas quickly. Find someone who is very comfortable taking directions from the team, listening to ideas without judging the approach, and is inherently limited in their ability to overdesign the prototype.

PROTOTYPING TOOLS

Tools affect the ability to prototype quickly and effectively. In some ways, a pencil is the ideal prototyping tool. It is useful for sketching ideas for any instructional approach. It can write over and erase. It's fast and inexpensive. It has a very low learning curve. Whiteboards and markers, flip charts, and other low technology aids can be excellent as well.

Moving up the technology path, there are now effective touch screen sketching tools that are easy to learn. They allow for quickly sketching, erasing, and modifying ideas, and projecting them for the team to review. They take varying amounts of time to learn, but most people can become proficient quickly. The prototyper shouldn't be learning to use the tool during iterative design cycles, of course, as it's important for prototypes to be produced quickly enough that they can be reviewed while the group is still assembled.

For e-learning, visual interactivity is a key aspect of design considerations. Animation, effects, controls, and input gestures are basic components of the learner experience and all have timing aspects that affect how they are perceived and how they contribute to the experience. When drawings are converted to functional software, they often produce interactive experiences that differ significantly from what was expected. While pencil sketches have value, they fall short in providing evidence of design suitability the team needs. Minimal levels of interactivity are required to evaluate alternative design ideas.

There are now many tools that support the rapid development of e-learning. They typically achieve speed by using templates or by optimizing for preset instructional paradigms. While these tools have their place, they may not provide the flexibility to explore a sufficiently wide range of instructional alternatives.

The capabilities of the prototyping tool can strongly affect how the team thinks, what possibilities are considered, and what opportunities go unrecognized. Choosing the wrong prototyping tool can mean choosing the wrong instructional approach.

PowerPoint as a Prototyping Tool

I am often asked about the effectiveness of using PowerPoint as a rapid prototyping tool. While many people have some familiarity with it and it is readily available as part of the Microsoft Office suite, I don't promote its use for prototyping (or e-learning in general) with enthusiasm.

Presentation tools support creation and delivery of presentations. They are nearly always honed for linear content presentation, rather than interactive, individualized, user experiences. As a prototyping tool, presentation tools limit the interactivity most prototypers can build or simulate. So, even if the design team proposes clever interactivity, the prototype built in a presentation tool is not likely to provide a suitable means of evaluating it.

Sure, folks can create some custom animations and transitions from one slide to the next, but we probably shouldn't be talking about slides in the first place. If the prototyper is unsure how to build an interactive element, given the need for speed, she is likely to compromise the design idea or employ an alternative approach. Neither of these fulfills the requirements of useful prototyping.

In summary, the prototyping tools the team chooses should provide the opportunity to partially implement a variety of designs quickly. Prototypes should be presented to the team in a form that can be revised quickly and with very little effort. Revision is expected and desired. Prototypers can use different tools either based on their personal skills or based on the appropriateness of the tool to the type of learning experience being considered. Linear tools should be used with great caution when prototyping interactive experiences.

A Private Word to Prototypers

Prototypers are the unsung heroes of a Savvy Start. And, like most heroes, they have a tough but vitally important job to do. If you are responsible for prototyping, you will hear the team discussing a lot of ideas and they will give you vague and probably conflicting directions on what to prototype. Almost as soon as you start you will mostly likely have questions about details that weren't discussed. Don't worry. You should feel free to fill in the blanks and do whatever you need to do that will help the team visualize their design in application. While you shouldn't deliberately misinterpret what they wanted to explore, the process of rapid prototyping is important because different people do—almost always—visualize verbally communicated designs differently. Prototypes are so helpful because they surface differences in expectations, and through iteration help groups come to common expectations and consensus.

It is easy to commit to a design idea too soon and miss the unexpected twists that come from brainstorming. Where you can, try to be true to the group's design of interest. Even if you have had a lot of experience with successful instructional approaches, hold your input and judgment back to let the group explore their ideas and work through the successes and failures that come along. If you have some suggestions, feel free to create an alternative prototype to be shown after the group reviews their design in prototype. The more prototypes, the better.

Brainstorming is a collaborative process, and not all groups brainstorm effectively. The room is purposefully filled with people who bring different viewpoints. With all of the challenges of group brainstorming—the chemistry of the people, the place, and the time allotted—everyone needs to feel their contributions were welcome and heard. Sometimes you have to prototype something you're quite opposed to so that the team can see why an idea wasn't really a good one. You should attempt to make the most of each idea. In doing so, the problems of bad ideas will become crystal clear.

More Tips on Brainstorming and Prototyping

It's a back and forth process: some brainstorming (but not too much) and some prototyping (but not too much). Small steps avoid unnecessary investment in dead-end ideas.

Don't go too far too soon—When the group gets their momentum going, it may be tough to keep them from attempting to design the entire learning product. But diving deeply into the content or tackling too much of it limits the creative consideration of primary alternatives. It's better to begin with small chunks—hopefully, chunks that are representative of larger segments of content. This practice will enable the team to be creative and to share their thoughts. Later you can encourage the team to brainstorm on how to bind smaller chunks into larger learning events.

Less content is better—Promote the idea of less content and more active opportunities to learn and apply new skills is almost always better than a lot of content with minimal learning activity. *But people need to know* all *these things.* Do they? Or has it simply been traditional to include superfluous content? Provide any concerned team members this comfort: Additional content, where it's truly needed, can and will be blended in later as activities and learning contexts require it. If, at the end of the process, there are content items that haven't been selected, it's likely that this content can be eliminated or made available as a reference tool.

Hopefully, the team will accept your recommendation and avoid lengthy discussions about the utility of every potential content element. You want to keep the focus of discussions and brainstorming on the learning experiences and the learning they promote, not on content nuances.

Don't design the final product—In addition to the tendency to prototype too much, the team may also want to design in detail. Details do make a difference, but the brainstorming team should be focusing on large design issues and major paradigms, not refinements. Quantity is better at this point than thoroughness.

Mistakes make magic—Making mistakes (and lots of them) is the magic of prototyping. Most of us want to create everything perfectly the first time, but that's just not realistic. Prototypes allow us to see how things might work, what makes sense, and where there's room for improvement. Use prototypes as a sandbox in which to make mistakes quickly and early so that they can be recognized and won't be costly later. Encourage the team to be creative without worrying about making mistakes!

Building the foundation for the prototype may include the team listing all of the contexts, challenges, activities, or feedback opportunities that the team can come up with quickly. The team only needs to think of some representative objectives, performance contexts, challenges, and activities. They are brainstorming, not designing. Omissions are expected and even necessary to use the available time wisely. They will be filled in when additional design work is done and content development begins in earnest.

STARTING TO BUILD YOUR PROTOTYPE

The designer and the prototyper need time to construct the prototype(s) the group has discussed. Other group members can take a break, check email, make phone calls, or just stretch their legs while prototypes are being built as rapidly as possible. The designer and prototyper need to be free of group discussion to synthesize and create. There is much to accomplish in little time.

The full group may be scheduled to return after a preset time, such as in 45 minutes, or be on call. While there needs to be adequate time to construct the prototype, SAM intentionally allows little time to construct each prototype. Prototypes need to be rough to prevent acceptance based on the heavy effort invested or because they weren't completed in time to discuss them.

A pragmatic consideration is that giving the team too much away time can allow some to become sidetracked in other activities, resulting in a dwindling team unable to reach the vital consensus of all stakeholders. To keep from spending too much time in prototyping and also to prevent team members from drifting away, it can be best to preset the time to reassemble. All participants should agree to be back on time.

For larger projects there can be two or more prototyping teams. This allows the brainstorming and design team to continue working while prototypers step out to work concurrently. Although not for beginners, large experienced teams can find this process keeps people productive and fully engaged.

Build an Instructional Event

There are many ways to construct a prototype quickly and effectively. The team's prototyper may have previously assembled a basic framework or have some components to choose from and combine. The instructional designer may have outlined a design that needs to be illustrated and built out a bit. There may be some existing materials or models that just need some modification or infusion of new content.

Rapid prototyping can be performed by a single individual with broad skills or a small team usually limited to no more than three: the project leader, an instructional designer, and the prototyper.

Typical Rapid Prototyping Session Agenda	
3–5 minutes	Determine the prototype(s) to be constructed.
2–3 minutes	Decide who will do what and when it will be finished.
25–30 minutes	Construct the prototype(s) and write choices/feedback.
1 minute	Have a quick progress check.
5 minutes	Review prototypes.
5 minutes	Make any necessary revisions and call the group back.

The goal is to create one or more prototypes that instantiate the team's design ideas. If it's a classroom activity, the prototype materials should be sufficient that the team can actually enact the activity as instructor and learners might do it. If it's an e-learning activity, some parts of the learner input gestures should be active so the courseware responses can be witnessed.

Not a lot can be accomplished in the short amount of time allowed and there will always be more the designer and prototyper would like to do. In nearly all cases, however, a rough and incomplete prototype is all that's needed for the group to determine if the design is going in a desired direction or if another approach really needs to be tried. If the results aren't conclusive, another round of prototyping under the team's direction is likely to do it.

REVIEW THE PROTOTYPE

Group members will be excited to see what has resulted from their discussions. Responses may range from extreme enthusiasm to disappointment. During the review of the prototype, all reactions are welcome and helpful. They represent greater project insight and are a step forward, regardless of how positive or negative.

Perhaps the worst outcome in prototype review is a hesitant, irresolute response from the group. While it's easy to confirm or discard a design based on intense reactions, muted responses fail to provide direction. Not to worry, SAM handles even this outcome comfortably, because even if the group's response was euphoric, the process imposes the challenge of setting the current design aside and composing another. It's very common that a design winning unanimous appeal is superseded by one that's even more appealing.

Review the Prototype Quickly

Depending on whether the prototyping is being done in the Savvy Start or iterative design, it is usually necessary to keep prototype reviews to no more than 45 minutes to an hour—even shorter, if possible.

In the Savvy Start, prototyping is about allowing key stakeholders to consider alternative approaches, consider available resources, and determine project preferences and guidelines. Much design work will be done in subsequent phases, so design is not really the primary outcome objective; rather, it's confirming backgrounding information and answering such key project questions as who is in charge, who is essential to achieving project success, and so on. So Savvy Start prototype reviews must transition quickly into *What else should we try? How can we overcome the biggest concerns about this prototype?*

In the iterative design phase, more time can and should usually be spent reviewing prototypes. More time will have been spent preparing these prototypes as more detailed issues are being explored with each iteration. Each successive prototype will be less about looking for entirely new approaches and more about deciding exactly what the design will be.

Prototype Walkthrough

Since prototypes are skeletal expressions of learning products, the team will need to be walked through each one, giving some guidance and direction to skip over incomplete or nonfunctioning components. As a way of developing a picture of the user experience, the prototyper may direct attention: *Let's say the instructor has just explained… After the e-learner has incorrectly chosen…*

The prototype presenter shouldn't rationalize or justify the design as the prototype is being presented. Other than explaining what would happen when the prototype is missing text, visuals, or functionality, the presenter should let the prototype stand on its own. The team needs to be experiencing the design to the extent possible, without commentary learners wouldn't have.

As the group discusses what they like and don't like, the leader creates a list of discussion points on a flip chart, whiteboard, or projected computer document. No time is taken to reach consensus; rather, focus remains on the experience provided by the prototype. These points initialize the evaluation component of the cycle to come next.

Evaluate

After the group has reviewed all of the prototypes, they return to the list of discussion points to determine what should be improved, revised, or removed from the prototype for the next iteration. Always keeping the learning objectives in mind, the team considers whether each of their dislikes is a design flaw, a content error, or possibly just a misunderstanding by the prototyper.

Unanticipated Discoveries

During the review of prototypes, especially during the Savvy Start, the team will reflect on many of the variables involved. *Do our students do their homework? Do our employees have convenient access to mobile devices? How many different languages do we need to include? Are coaches available in all locations? How often does the content change?*

Background information used to initially define the project may be incorrect or incomplete. The delivery means assumed to be appropriate may not seem so appropriate anymore, or multiple means may now appear to be necessary. The group may well consider the need to change the targeted behavior outcomes during the review of the prototype.

Such considerations have traditionally been part of the ADDIE analysis phase. These are considerations important to any development process. The foundation needs to be correct or the structure built on it will be ineffective. Prototyping is perhaps a disguised, but nevertheless highly effective, way of asking the questions that make sure critical considerations occur. When the team asks itself whether a prototyped solution will work, it's natural to reconsider the assumptions upon which a design is based. Such reconsideration is vital early in the process, and with SAM, it typically happens much faster with more accuracy and communication in the context of considering the rather specific learning activities represented by prototypes. But to be sure, it's important not to blindly build successive prototypes without stepping back during their evaluation to be sure the solutions being considered are appropriate in every way.

User Feedback

Even the most talented learning design team is handicapped in its capacity to define the best experiences for a select group of learners because they aren't those learners. Thinking and reacting as a person without the knowledge and skills you have is far more difficult than it appears. With prototypes available so early in the process, SAM provides the invaluable opportunity to get reactions from both recent learners and representative learners. This process difference alone may be sufficient reason to abandon ADDIE.

The traditional ISD approach calls for learner access to learning products after analysis, design, and development (in some instance, not until after implementation as well). That is, learner responses and evaluation aren't gathered until the products are very nearly complete. Of course, ADDIE can be modified to include learner interaction much earlier. That makes a significant improvement. But many organizations fear that by having learners review an incomplete application, great anxiety and confusion will ensue. There is too often a concern that nothing can be gained from inexperienced users this early in the process.

Most of this apprehension is due to the design and development approaches being used. If specification documents are being used to convey the initial design, learners will be challenged to provide any meaningful input. These are often complex documents that are meant to communicate design approaches between experienced instructional designers and developers. They are not meant to be used by learners.

Advantageously, with SAM, everyone can have early access to prototypes that support a more authentic learning experience. And there is so much to gain when there remains in-budget flexibility to make changes. Learner reviews early in the process provide a vital validation of design assumptions that can so easily be off. The SAM design team uses prototypes to challenge their initial assumptions, and interaction with learners provides another level of design challenge and validation.

During learner review, it's important not to editorialize about the design, but it is necessary to explain what is intentionally missing and incomplete so learners won't flounder or think they are misunderstanding. Delaying such explanation, however, until the learner makes inquiries is often the best approach. To the extent possible, learners should experience prototyped learning events as genuine learning events.

Checking designs with learners should occur often during the process, not just at the beginning or end. Reviews in the prototype stage will provide insight into the fundamental design, while later reviews will help to test wording, instructions, illustrations, interface, navigation, feedback, and so on. Involving learners at every stage of design and development benefits product design and helps ensure effectiveness.

WRAP UP

Prototypes are simple in design and functionality and provide a means of conducting analysis cost-effectively, stimulating creative design, and gaining learner evaluation and perspectives very early in the process. The advantages of successive approximation become apparent through the iterative production and review of prototypes.

CHAPTER 10

Setting the Target

Projects have a purpose, a goal, a criterion for success. It's not always clear what the goal is, but it's not safe to make assumptions about what it is or about whether key stakeholders have the same goal for the project. Even assuming that the goal is about performance outcomes is risky.

It's important for overall success—and all the decisions that have to be made to realize success—to know what the target actually is and how success will be measured. Successive approximation, pragmatic as always, helps flesh out what people are thinking, define the goal, and determine the most efficient way of reaching the target.

GOALS

Goals often evolve and sometimes even transform into something entirely different from what was initially set. Up until this point, the process has encouraged creativity over either practicality or appropriateness. *Everything goes in brainstorming.* The team hasn't had to stifle creativity, worry about budget, or consider much about the limitations of delivery. This may seem backward, as traditional processes and even common sense would suggest that setting the goal is the very first thing to do.

Ready, fire, aim. Even with successive approximation, some discussion about goals is likely and appropriate from the very first cycle of the Savvy Start, but no one was appointed judge to determine whether each idea was fully in-line with both constraints and the project target. This looseness is deliberate, because experimenting with alternate solutions can actually be one of the best ways of determining what the goal should be. Getting the goal right is, of course, extremely important, and while contrary to intuition, finalizing the goal shouldn't be the first thing to do; neither should it be the last.

Goal setting in SAM is, like the whole of the process, an iterative process that might best be viewed as piggybacking on instructional design. As the team excitedly explores ideas for learning experiences, some ideas will expand thoughts of what skills might be targeted while conversely, initially appealing design ideas may spend too much time on insignificant outcomes. It's unfortunate when goals are set too soon and opportunities, perhaps the most valuable opportunities, are bypassed by strict adherence to initial goals. On the other hand, it is important to implant goals before the following steps of additional design and major development work begin.

After several iterations of design, prototyping, and evaluation, it is time to consider project constraints, requirements, and goals in earnest. A tested and effective way of doing this is by writing clear and concise outcome objectives, assigning treatment methods to each objective, and deciding how to assess success.

INSTRUCTIONAL OBJECTIVES

Objectives are needed for estimating the amount of work to be done, preparing cost estimates, listing needed resources, setting out a project schedule, and, in short, doing many of the project planning tasks ahead. Instructional objectives provide a helpful foundation for design and development; however, not everyone is familiar with writing formal objectives and this may cause them to be put off or feel unable to contribute. In actuality, a review of constructed prototypes may well reveal the knowledge and behavioral skills the team has found to be of primary importance. With just a little guidance, the team can distill what they've been saying into objectives. Writing the objectives after some prototyping has been completed is a more interesting and engaging task, helps the team determine if they've been on an appropriate track, and provides support and guidance for the continued iterations.

Objectives clarify exactly what should be taught and learned. Good objectives have very little ambiguity in them, although as tightly constructed as one may try to make them, there is often more

> Although this book is about process and not design, preparation of objectives, the objectives x treatments matrix, and in-line assessments are important steps in the process. We divert to design topics a bit here to talk about these essential activities primarily as a clarification of the process.

opportunity for varied interpretations than intended. Here is an example objective and some reminders of how to write them.

Sample behavioral objective:
Within 30 minutes of arriving on site and without any errors or omissions, pool service personnel will perform all routine cleaning items, test and treat water, replace all owner furniture and equipment as found, place all service equipment and unused supplies back in the truck, and leave a properly written, dated, and signed service ticket at the front door as described in the company's best practices guidebook.

Complete behavioral objectives have three components (reference the example objective above):

1. A description of observable behavior (perform routine cleaning, etc.)
2. The conditions under which the learner must be able to perform successfully (within 30 minutes of arriving on site, on site with a service truck, etc.)
3. Criterion of successful behavior (without any errors or omissions)

Verbs such as "think," "understand," and "know" are not observable (or measurable) behaviors, whereas "list," "identify," "complete" and many others are. Even if the intent is to stimulate cognitive functions, such as appreciating, understanding, or feeling, it's important for designers to express observable manifestations of such mental behavior so that we can assess whether or not the instruction is having the needed impact.

Objectives x Treatments Matrix

An important use of objectives is to determine how many types of instructional events or "treatments" will need to be designed for the entire application. All objectives need design treatments—one or more—but not all objectives need to have unique pedagogical designs. Preparing a matrix of objectives and instructional designs gives the team insight into what design work has been accomplished and what remains to be done.

Typically, the team writes objectives in the first column of a table. When instructional designs are sketched, each one is lettered and briefly described at the top of columns. As the team takes up successive objectives, they look to see whether one or more existing designs would constitute good and appropriate learning events for them. If so, they check that cell of the growing matrix to note use of the existing design and move on to other objectives (see Table 10-1).

Table 10-1. Objectives x Treatments Matrix Summary

Instructional Treatments

		A	B	C	D
Objectives	**1**	✓			
	2		✓		
	3	✓	✓		
	4	✓	✓		
	5	✓		✓	
	6	✓			✓

Building the matrix will be instructive to the team, and it will help them see how objectives are used to estimate the amount of effort it will take to complete the entire project. At this point in the process, however, it's not necessary to write the full complement of objectives, even if you could. Just write a few so that you can select a couple for prototyping and demonstrate the process that will be continued later.

Table 10-2. Example Objectives x Treatments Matrix

Observable Behavior	Treatment	
	Context	**Activity**
1. Clear pool area for safety and proper cleaning.	On site, at a variety of pools: Some situations show hazards (such as children playing nearby, gardeners at work, or party preparations with electrical devices near water) and typical obstacles to cleaning (chairs, tables, glasses, etc.).	(A) Target identification and classification: Find all items of concern and match with appropriate remedy.

Observable Behavior	Treatment	
	Context	Activity
2. Test pool water.	Provided: a basic residential sanitizer residual and pH testing kit with color-coded directions for testing DPD chlorine (.5–5 ppm), DPD bromine (1–10 ppm) and pH (6.8–8.2). Pools have normal and abnormal water conditions.	(B) Sequential task completion: Procedural activity simulation for common errors in processes with delayed feedback. Learners must perform test steps in proper order and report correct results.
3. Examine water filter. Clean or replace.	Different types of filters (sand, D.E., or cartridge) and filter conditions (normal, damaged, spent).	(A) Target identification and classification: Find all items of concern and match with appropriate remedy. (B) Remedy: Sequential task completion.
4. Clean pool.	Pools with varying states of debris, tile calcification, and water clarity.	(A) Target identification and classification. (B) Sequential task completion.
5. Clean site.	Pool areas previously shown for objective #1 after cleaning with both service equipment and customer property in likely places.	(A) Target identification. (C) Drag and drop positioning: Place objects in original positions, safe positions, or truck as appropriate.
6. Complete service ticket.	Completed forms corresponding to performed service but with errors.	(A) Target identification. (D) Text entry correction.

In the example, objectives 1, 3, 4, 5, and 6 can all be reached or assisted with the help of target identification activities. Sequential task completion is also used for multiple objectives (2, 3, and 4). The objectives x treatment matrix helps designers employ the efficiency of reusing an instructional model. It won't be necessary to prototype repeated uses of instructional treatments (and developers will be able to reuse model to cover spans of content). Only one prototype is needed for each type of objective and activity, not for each objective.

Working Backward

The natural instinct is to work from the simple and basic to the complex and advanced skills. While SAM supports this traditional sequence as well as any other, some find persuasive benefits from working the other way; that is, from the final or "terminal" objectives backward to the foundational or beginning objectives. I personally find working backward helps me focus on what's most important and use my resources most effectively.

To work backward, the question to be asked repeatedly is this: *What are the last skills we want learners performing successfully before…?* In the first iteration, the question is, *What are the last skills we want learners performing before we award them their completion certificate and release them to the world?* This question is answered easily. We want them performing the tasks the instruction was designed to teach. We want them successfully performing in contexts and situations that are identical to the contexts and situations they will actually face, or as close to them as we can possibly simulate.

Filling in the objectives x treatments matrix, we would begin with objectives that define the ultimate performance targeted. We would then design the learning experiences that would support this performance and remediate when learners failed to reach the criterion. Then we would ask the question again, *What are the last skills we want learners performing before we assign them this last instructional event?* Our answers would create the learning objectives that, in delivery sequence, would precede the objective currently in the matrix. We would look to see if the instructional treatments existing for any objective would be applicable to these new objectives, with adjustments to context and content, of course. If the treatments appear satisfactory, we simply check off the reuse of them and continue iterating the performance question. If not, then we would design the treatments needed and press onward—or backward! Eventually, the team will back into initial levels of performance abilities that all targeted learners are expected to have. And then stop.

PRE-EXISTING CONTENT

Working backward from desired performance outcomes is a very successful and highly recommended practice. Working backward from desired outcomes, defining performance objectives, and building the objectives x treatments matrix clarifies content that is and isn't needed in the product.

Working from existing content is, unfortunately, a more common practice—and a practice that leads in the wrong direction. It's true that content is expensive, and that time and money can be saved when existing content can be reused. It is very easy to underestimate the amount of time, effort, and cost required to develop good course content; not to mention the special talents needed to do it well. Poor content will ruin the product and prevent a successful learning experience.

Some designers consider a clear presentation of content to be a sufficient instructional strategy—an effective means of achieving the learning and performance outcomes. However, this approach works only in those situations where learners are highly motivated and where all that's necessary to perform is knowing how to do it. To learn more complex tasks— usually the more valuable tasks—people need to put new information to work within a meaningful context. And they need to practice. Maximum impact occurs when the volume of content is reduced and the focus is placed on a few key behaviors.

The objectives x treatments matrix should drive content requirements, but when there is a lot of pre-existing content, there tends to be a feeling that it needs to be used—pretty much all of it—so as not to be wasteful. Instructional designers face this situation frequently and know that large amounts of content must be whittled down into useful pieces. It's often more expedient to start from scratch.

Content is included to achieve objectives and for no other purpose. Extraneous content consumes too much time, even if just for presentation, and leaves little for learning and practice.

There's a second prevalent misunderstanding about pre-existing content that can be even more problematic. If the existing content were developed for one mode of delivery, such as a book, and the product being developed were for an instructor-led course, the existing content would be inadequate. It's not just that the format would be wrong. It would be necessary to rewrite what exists and add more content so that instructors could answer learner questions, perform demonstrations, and so on.

Figure 10-1 provides a visual representation of the transition of pre-existing information into content for an e-learning application.

Figure 10-1. Usefulness of Content Developed for Other Instructional Modes

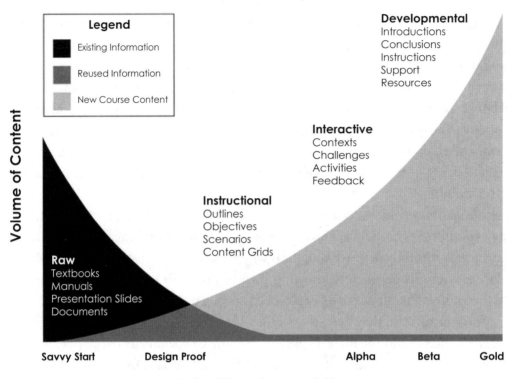

Notice that the project starts with a large amount of content that comes from existing manuals, presentation slides, documents, and other sources. This material is helpful in early project work and when only presentations intended for passive learning are being developed. But active learning events require context, challenge, activities, and feedback. Fragments of these content components may be found in existing materials, but development work often requires filling in the many gaps between what's available and what's needed. Content creation work may range from creating missing pieces to truly starting from scratch. The more interactive and the more individualized the product is to be, the more content will be needed. Again, it's a common mistake to underestimate the work needed to create content in the form needed, especially when pre-existing content is available.

Developing content for prototyped designs, as will take place in the iterative development phase, takes a substantial effort and should be given the necessary time and talent. The organization's desire to use much, if not all, of the existing content should be challenged. The learners will be served best with a few focused key points that will support their performance change efforts.

ASSESSMENT

Sponsors may show little interest in assessment except for post-tests, but learning events need interleaved assessments as a means of adapting the instruction to the learner, providing feedback, and determining the effectiveness of the instruction.

Macro Assessment

People think of post-tests when they think of assessment, but there's far more involved here. Classical post-tests generally have little value for any purpose, although it is traditional to award certificates and to issue grades based largely on post-test scores. Unfortunately, post-test measures provide incentives for learners to use only short-term memory in preparation for the test, resulting in rapid extinction of learned behaviors after the test. On-the-job practice can counter this loss, but delayed measures based on post-learning performance can be much more meaningful. At the same time, when anticipated by learners, delayed measures encourage sufficient practice to commit learning to long-term memory.

In any case, the design team needs the clear targets that assessments represent, and learners need the goals that assessments define. To prevent "teaching the test"—a situation in which learners are prepared only to perform well on post-tests and not in real performance situations—a separate team working in parallel may define assessment exercises. They work from the same set of objectives as the instructional design team, but the assessments are not shared with the instructional designers so that content developers will focus on preparing learners to fully meet the requirements of the objectives—not of just the tests. This is a rather extreme tactic and not necessary in many situations, but preparing criterion tasks that demonstrate competency and could be used for post-instruction assessment is a smart thing to do.

Learning projects exist to achieve behavioral change. The most vital, ultimate assessment is whether they do that. The most effective assessments are not post-tests, but rather on-the-job or in-real-life behaviors. In academic settings, teachers should be more satisfied and proud if a student were able to participate in an intelligent conversation on a subject of instruction with learned individuals than able to provide correct answers to test questions. In the business setting, trainers should be more satisfied when an employee corrects a mechanical malfunction efficiently rather than when he or she correctly answers test questions on how it should be done.

Micro Assessment

Each interaction with a learner is an opportunity for assessment. In a classroom context or synchronous remote learning, individual assessment interactions carry with them the potential pain of embarrassment. While some would argue that these challenges are motivating and learners should be able to withstand the pressures of public evaluation, it's often better to use more private forms of assessment.

Perhaps the biggest advantage of e-learning is that it can assess learner abilities and readiness at every point of private interaction. Each learner has the opportunity to work with the full attention of the mentor and make mistakes without jeers from peers. Interestingly, the four cornerstones of e-learning interaction, context, challenge, activity, and feedback, are the same essential components of sound assessments. Separate design and development is not needed to construct in-line assessments because instruction and assessment are designed and built together. Each interaction can be both a teaching and assessment event.

Ideally, interactions simultaneously give learners the cognitive stimulation they need to learn and instructors (or the instructional software) the information needed to guide the learner. By knowing where an individual learner's strengths and weaknesses lie, instructors can determine what the learner needs to learn and what they are ready to learn. Because instructors are usually working with many learners simultaneously in a classroom, they aren't able to craft individual learning plans that adapt quickly. Indeed, their instructional plans are often set before the term begins, and learners must keep up as best they can.

Individualization is a term for adapting learning experiences to people. It requires knowledge of people. Superficial but welcomed individualization includes:
- Using the learner's name in sentences: *Here are your options, Susan.*
- Recalling information: *Welcome back. You haven't missed a day since we started.*
- Reporting progress: *You have only two modules left to complete.*

More significant forms of individualization are tied to assessments, such as:
- Comparison to previous personal performance: *Your best performance yet, Eric! Excellent.*
- Comparison to others or to averages: *You required less time to solve this problem than nearly everyone else.*
- Branching based on performance need (e.g. remediation): *Let's back up a step and review another example.*
- Recognition of learning styles and abilities: *You're doing much better after viewing videos than after reading documents, so let's jump right to a video first.*
- Honoring preferences: *Since you've indicated you like challenges, let's see if you can solve this problem before we study the principles involved.*

In order to accomplish significant levels of individualization, it's important to design interactions that yield the prerequisite data. The SAM team can benefit from considering the value of individualization at the outset and then including necessary interactions and assessments to provide for them.

SUMMARY

Although we want to be creative and design learning experiences that are packed with energy and engagement, they have a purpose. Learning experiences are meant to build skills and change performance. It's therefore critical to the success of the creative, iterative process to set goals. Writing objectives helps articulate what the project intends to achieve and helps focus brainstorming efforts on appropriate needs.

The objectives x treatments matrix is a simple mechanism to help minimize the number of unique treatments that are designed, which in turn minimizes development time and costs.

Assessments, built of the same components as interactive learning experiences (context, challenge, activity, and feedback), are necessary within instructional interactions to provide meaningful individualization.

CHAPTER 11

Designing for Success

Process is about doing the right things at the right times. It's the formula for every kind of success, actually. And doing the right things begins with knowing what the right things are; then focusing on the right goals and tasks continually. If nothing else, successive approximation stresses the importance of alternatively focusing on the big picture, then on details of a learning experience, and then back again to the big picture, and so on. It's the purpose of iterations to take only small steps before evaluating whether they advance sufficiently toward the goal. Iterations aren't undertaken just for repetition or perfection of a component. They are undertaken to help make sure each component is justified by the goal and helpful to reaching it.

BREADTH VERSUS DEPTH

SAM stresses the use of sketches and the development of prototypes to minimize investment in any idea until there's certainty that the idea is 1) a good design in itself and 2) fits well with other designs. You can't be sure of fit, of course, until other ideas have been fleshed out. SAM designers therefore take new ideas only a short distance before setting them aside and addressing other content. In other words, they prefer to cover the full breadth of project content before diving into any designs to great depth.

Warning: It's extremely tempting to continue iterations to perfect ideas rather than move on to other content. Perhaps the biggest liability with SAM is that many people do not resist this temptation and dive into a design too deeply. Too much depth too soon can result in a variety of unfortunate outcomes including an overall catastrophe. Some of the likely problems are:

- uneven levels of refinement
- inconsistencies
- excluded essential content
- extravagant designs for relatively unimportant content
- inadequate attention to critical skills and behaviors
- incoherent courses.

A blended solution includes a variety of learning events supported and delivered in different ways. It requires consideration of how prototyped activities will be synchronized with other learning events. Mapping out the critical connections between them in detail is an instructional design activity in itself. As part of this effort, the team may consider including learner support tools such as a reference glossary, notebook, online links, contact information, or performance support applications on mobile devices. It may include technology for learners to communicate with and ask questions of others. Creating a successful overall design requires visibility of the whole.

LOOK AHEAD

Each time iterations cycle back to evaluation, it's another time to ascertain appropriateness of the most recent decisions and the foundations they lay for future steps. Within the Savvy Start, some members may be concerned that not all of the targeted behaviors have been covered or that there are design issues still remaining to be addressed. It may be helpful to refresh the context of the Savvy Start and the function of iterations within the overall process. It's not the purpose of the Savvy Start or any single iteration to deal with the entirety of the design needs.

After the Savvy Start and before moving on to complete additional design work with the revised post-savvy team, contributors unfamiliar with the process may need help gaining a better appreciation of how the Savvy Start work will be used going forward. Again, the need for visibility of the whole not withstanding, segmentation and iterations are the key solutions to all these concerns.

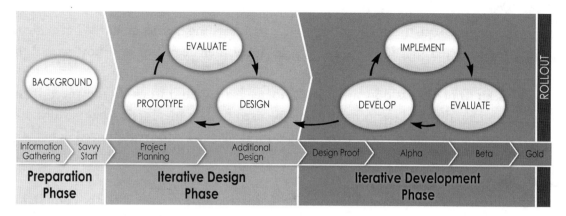

While the process may look complex, teams generally don't find it so. It's basically successive redeployment of only one structure of evaluation, design, and development.

Validation With Learners

Frequent evaluation provides assurance that the process will yield a successful result. While the team frequently evaluates their designs, much of the evaluation requires the availability of learners to test the evolving product. Scheduling participants for user testing can place an additional burden on the project, but the value is so great that the benefit far exceeds the inconvenience.

The mechanics of scheduling user testing often cause delays and are of sufficient effort that teams may delay and sometimes even forgo it. Known to be unwise to experienced users of SAM, skipping early validation of design ideas with actual learners often causes rework to be required after product introduction.

Refer to chapter 15 for more information on managing user reviews.

The Complete Solution

By exploring various solutions, the team will have a better sense of what's possible and what would work within their organization. While maintaining a focus on the overall goal of organizational and individual success, the team will examine the project's target numerous times. But the project may still need more definition of what is necessary to create the complete, desired solution. Some additional, helpful questions include:

- What information do you want to know as learners work through the learning experiences? For example, do you want to know what errors they make, what comments they have, what options or tools they used?

- What evidence can the application provide that learning has occurred? What evidence can be collected that learners are able to apply their learning, and how would this be done?
- What kinds of reports do you want? Who needs them and when do they need them? Can some individual performance data be used to help mentors? What performance data need to be kept private? How secure does collected information need to be?

Compliancy Issues

Preparing learners for certification, building exercises that work with confidential information, or training performance that has significant liabilities (surgical procedures, commercial airline piloting) leads to compliancy issues. There may be a requirement that the application be made available for access by physically impaired individuals. If e-learning is involved, there may also be LMS interface compliancy issues or the necessity to comply with certain technical standards.

It is helpful to get answers to these questions as soon as possible. Backgrounding research may provide the answers, but there may still be open questions and often are.

Performance Tracking

Collecting data items necessary for specified assessments may require supportive networking and database management capabilities. Most often this is determined by the capabilities of an LMS. While an LMS usually provides data collection, tracking, and reporting, the specific ability of an LMS may not match the assessment collection strategy that a project requires. For example, if the team decides to create a series of independent modules instead of a single combined course, learners may not be able to reference their progress or success across modules.

There are many options that are available to the team in their design efforts, but knowing what is available with the LMS or data tracking system that must be used, if any, will help to reduce unnecessary or unsupportable design decisions. Unfortunately, restrictive firewalls or confidentiality issues and policies may prevent required user log in or collection of certain data that might be just what's needed for an ideal learning activity.

Media

Media (audio, graphics, illustrations, photographs, animation, and so on) are important tools for creating impactful learning experiences. Media can convey specific concepts in a way that creates a vivid or emotional impact on the learner, which in turn may enhance motivation and retention.

Media also affect the sense of quality and may determine such things as perceived seriousness of the content or excitement an organization wishes to communicate. A game-like interface may suggest that learners should be having fun, while a childish interface may communicate a misunderstanding or even disrespect for learners or the content. Organizational culture and existing style guides often have a bearing on the selection of media, and sometimes set requirements that are much easier to comply with if recognized from the project's start.

Although the course's effectiveness is determined by its ability to produce the desired performance change, there is no doubt that it will also be judged by how it looks. Often it's the case that projects are judged heavily by how they look. Fortunately, learners also have more positive expectations of e-learning that has visual appeal, a positive spirit, and engaging energy.

The selection of media treatments is an important consideration in the process, not only because of its ability to engage learners, but also because media will affect both the cost of the project and the options for designing the interactions. For example, the use of certain media may be limited by projection equipment in the classroom, cost of printing in color, or the bandwidth of the organization's network. The design team needs to be mindful of making sure they do not set unrealistic expectations for product delivery.

CHAPTER 12

Project Planning

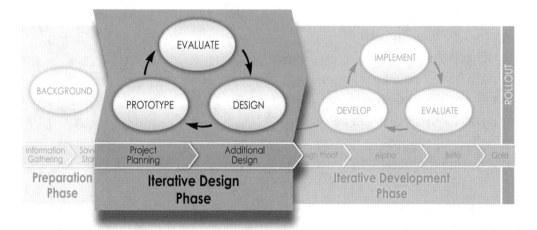

In the post-savvy, iterative design phase, there are many loose ends that need to be tied up. Design continues following the same process as in the Savvy Start, although usually with a select team to speed things along and reduce costs. But, most importantly, there is planning to do.

In this chapter we will cover the following topics, which are essential to project planning:
- discussing expectations versus budget constraints
- identifying project costs
- defining the delivery platform
- addressing limitations
- creating a well-documented plan.

INITIAL PLANNING

Rapid collaborative design serves as the foundation to the successive approximation process. Bringing a team together to create quick and ugly prototypes starts the ball rolling toward an effective and engaging learning product. Iteration is the strategy from beginning to end; however, this flexible, creative process must usually produce a product by a certain date, do so within a budget, and produce acceptable results. That's the role of planning.

It's unfortunate that limitations are often set before the Savvy Start is finished. They are often set even before the project starts. While the SAM process is extremely good for fitting projects within preset constraints and producing the best possible product within them, it cannot overcome totally inappropriate constraints.

At the completion of the Savvy Start, enough information is known, and known for the first time, to determine mostly:
- the right content
- the right instructional paradigm
- the right modes of delivery
- the right resources that will be needed
- the right budget range
- the right amount of time to allow for project design and development.

This is a prime decision point. Can and should the project be properly funded and resourced? Or should less (or more) ambitious goals be set? Or should the project be aborted?

Although there needs to be flexible creativity in the project, the ability to manage for success depends on a structured plan that clarifies what needs to happen, when it will happen, who will make it happen, and how it will happen.

After the completion of the Savvy Start, it's time in the SAM process to begin developing a formal project plan.

Priorities

Priorities help a lot. With only a month to complete a project, it probably couldn't have many highly complex learning events. With a limited budget, the team may have to choose between professional illustrations and clip art. When resources are limited, multiple uses of designs may be necessary. But when costs of performance errors are high, impact is essential. When learners speak different languages or are a part of different cultures, localization is a requirement. Trade-offs are nearly always necessary. Will it be high-end media, numerous interactions, professional writing, quick completion, low cost, or any number of other project choices?

Realistic plans are built on compromises, and priorities are vital to setting the right ones. Setting priorities early in the project is also a great way for everyone on the design team to create and maintain expectations. To begin formalizing what is known about constraints and declaring priorities, necessary qualities or parameters of the following key components should be defined and then placed in rank order:

- timeline (schedule)
- media
- interactivity
- content
- instructional design
- budget
- partnerships (collaboration)
- reviews and approvals.

The team should be sure to add missing components that are important to the particular project and circumstances.

SAM Project Manager Tip:

Tape the list to the wall for reference throughout the remainder of the meeting. Send every team member a copy of this list after the meeting. Later in the project, refer back to this list especially prior to the design proof and alpha release. Having clear expectations and priorities will help to keep your team on track during each of the upcoming reviews. More importantly, these priorities will help guide the team through the project planning activities.

Project Costs

After the Savvy Start has been completed, there is a good basis for estimating how much the entire project is going to cost, what resources will need to be available, and how long it's going to take. While there may be pressure—as there is in many organizations—to determine a budget early in the process, even before the Savvy Start, doing so is truly unwise. It's like asking how much a wedding will cost without knowing how many attendees are expected, where it is to be held, whether it's formal or informal, whether dinner is to be served, and so on. Until an objectives x treatments matrix has been constructed, it's very hard to estimate how many different treatments will have to be used, how deep the content information will have to be, what media will be essential, and so on.

The range of possible costs is simply too large to have any value. The Savvy Start provides answers which, together with backgrounding information, a commitment of critical resources (such as SMEs, supervisors, and learners), and the new prototypes, narrow the range of possible costs and make it possible to provide well-founded estimates.

Hopefully, by this point in the process, the team is convinced that creating something ineffective will be the most costly path to take. Unfortunately, there may be a predetermined and inappropriate budget, probably too small, of course. If the budget cannot be expanded, it's back to the priorities and compromises with the hope that it will be possible to do something effective. The usual solution is to reduce content to the core of what's really needed and not less. Alternatively, a phased approach may be the best option. Each phase might be done well enough to achieve effectiveness on selected topics and justify similar investments later for remaining content.

When schedules and costs are not predicated on a Savvy Start, guesswork is at play and some red flags should be raised. Of course, it's possible to build learning solutions within a very wide cost range, but the solutions at opposite ends of the range do not have equal effectiveness nor the same return-on-investment. Underestimating the costs will likely create solutions that are so ineffective that the entire investment is at risk. Consequences include wasted learner time, lost opportunities to iterate and implement effective solutions, and learners becoming frustrated or disengaged with the effort needed to succeed. Launching an ineffective program is damaging and expensive.

Knowing initial cost expectations is important, although it's best if expectations are not formed until after a Savvy Start can inform them.

Delivery Platform

When remote learning or e-learning is being considered, it is essential to define the delivery platform capabilities and constraints as soon as possible. Determine if systems can support high-end graphics, sound effects, streaming video, animation, real-time communications, and so on. The design of the final application will be affected greatly by platform capabilities— even what might at first seem like minor limitations, so determining what is possible should be done before further design efforts are undertaken.

In e-learning the limitations or opportunities offered by the delivery system fall into two basic areas: the individual hardware, such as laptops or mobile devices, and the network. Although the cost of capable multimedia computers is miniscule in comparison to the cost of wasted learner time and the costs of poorly trained performers, it can be difficult in both corporate and academic institutions to upgrade hardware as necessary to support optimal learning experiences.

As we move toward a more distributed environment with browser-based applications and tools, the impact of software versioning is also a necessary limitation to the learner's systems. Many of today's development platforms offer new and exciting methods for creating and presenting multimedia content. However, delivery of these applications and the output they offer may be beyond the limitation of the learners' browser or device.

Some designs will not be viable if the delivery platform doesn't have access to high-speed communications as learners work. For example, if learners will be involved in multi-player games, computers will need to be networked and have uninterrupted access. If the instructional design provides exercises based on each learner's growing competencies, records of the learner's response history must be available to the computer, even if the learner uses a different computer for each session.

PRAGMATIC CONSIDERATIONS

SME Access and Content

Experts are often very busy people. Those who hold the standards for an organization's best practices and those most esteemed for both their knowledge and teaching abilities in educational institutions are often busy with an extraordinary workload. While these very people may be among the most enthusiastic supporters of training and development, their involvement in a time-sensitive project is often problematic. Development teams frequently list delayed access to SMEs and delayed approvals as the primary cause of budget and schedule overruns.

It's always important to remember that content developed for one form of instructional delivery, such as instructor-led classroom instruction, is not sufficient for other forms— especially for interactive instruction, where the invention of learning experiences and providing learners the opportunities to make mistakes and learn from them requires much more content depth.

Project Teams, Approvals, Decision Making

With the experience gained by the end of the Savvy Start, the team usually develops a unique relationship and forms thoughts about how everyone can work together for project success. But the select group willing and able to participate in this start-up phase is not likely to continue at the same pace working through additional design, planning, and development. Part of good project planning takes into account who will be continuing and what new players will need to do to catch up and become productive.

Again—and most important—are the issues of getting approvals and decisions made. It's easy for an organization to demand delivery at a certain time, such as readiness for school opening in the fall or the scheduled time of a new product launch, and then delay the timely completion of reviews and approvals without warning. Planning needs to consider whether there is an authority ready to assure reviews and approvals occur as scheduled or whether there is likely to be slack that can delay the project and run up costs.

If the scope of the project changes, who will approve the changes and budgetary ramifications, if any? If an approval is late, who has the authority to obtain it or approve a change to the project schedule? It's smart to solidify problem resolution measures to be taken as part of project planning—while project enthusiasm is high and no project problems are on the table.

Responsibilities

Who is (and is not) going to be able take responsibilities for continuing roles? The project manager needs to be wary of delegation that removes real decision makers from the process. Major problems may result because the person who steps back and isn't involved closely may retain the power to veto decisions made by his or her delegate. When people do not fully understand why decisions were made, vetoes can cause problematic delays or poor direction.

Documentation

Many organizations have expectations, whether defined formally or historically, for how projects are to be documented and managed. In any case, having a well-documented project plan is important and a topic deserving an expanded discussion beyond the scope of this book. There are many available resources devoted to this topic, including my own (Allen and Lipshutz, in press). We note herein when and where project planning is appropriately undertaken in successive approximations and provide an example plan for guidance (see pages 134–156).

Figure 12-1 demonstrates an effective way to visualize the start dates for each of the steps in the SAM process.

Figure 12-1. SAM Project Start Dates

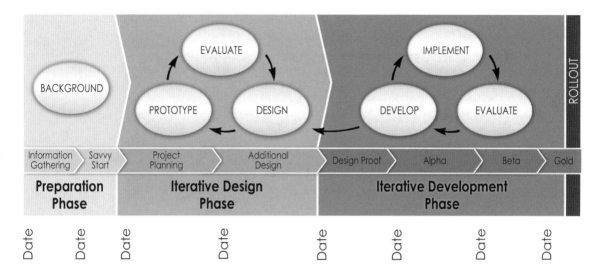

However, having solid start dates is only one aspect of the type of information you will need and want to document during your SAM project. Included on the following pages is a sample project document created for a mock course development. Note this project document not only includes project milestones and deliverables, but also incorporates into a single document the business need, performance challenges, learner needs and instructional treatments to address these needs. It reveals much of the work undertaken in good project planning and provides a framework for it.

Sample Project Plan
e-Learning Training for Statistical Process Control at ABC Company

TABLE OF CONTENTS

PROJECT OVERVIEW
Business Problem
Performance Gap
The Solution
ABC Company Vision / Mission Statement
ABC Company Criteria for Success

DESIGN AND DEVELOPMENT PROCESS

CONTENT & OBJECTIVES X TREATMENT MATRIX
Matrix
Instructional Treatments

MANAGING SCOPE
Defined Scope
Scope Change Management

QUALITY
User Testing Plan
Quality Assurance/Quality Compliance
Scope of Quality Assurance

PROJECTED MILESTONES & DELIVERABLES

ROLES & RESPONSIBILITIES
General Responsibilities
Project Sponsor
Development Team

DECISION MAKING
Approval

COMMUNICATIONS PLAN AND ISSUE RESOLUTION
Primary Contact Responsibility
Project Status
Email Protocol
Course Comments & Fixes
Meeting Planning
Best Practices
File Transfer
Project Webpage
Issue Resolution

PROJECT RISKS

Project Overview

Business Problem

In order to maintain its high design and product development quality standards, ABC Company has a recurring need to train new employees and re-educate its existing employees on basic Statistical Process Control (SPC) techniques and the benefits of using SPC in a manufacturing or engineering environment. Currently, ABC Company teaches this content in instructor-led classes at its main training center. The current course content needs to be updated as many of the underlying SPC forms have changed, needs to be translated into three languages for employees outside the U.S., and the Quality Assurance department must meet a surge in demand for this training based on new quality initiatives that ABC Company is rolling out in six months.

Analysis of the related needs of ABC Company stakeholders during the initial analysis and design cycle (referred to as the "Savvy Start") is reported in the Savvy Summary Report.

Performance Gap

All engineering and manufacturing employees of ABC Company must be able to analyze and / or apply SPC techniques in their job roles. Thirty percent (30%) of the existing employees are not using SPC correctly or at all. ABC Company is re-focusing efforts on quality in all its manufacturing and engineering operations in the U.S. and abroad and wants its employees to possess the skills to properly use SPC.

The Solution

ABC Company has determined that use of a comprehensive multimedia-based computer training course will provide the most cost and instructionally effective method of training a diverse group of ABC Company employees (titles and roles) in SPC principles and techniques.

The course will consist of various lessons that will include highly interactive instructional elements to engage learners and increase their correct use of SPC principles in their work. This course while primarily designed for ABC Company employees will also be made available to ABC Company suppliers looking to hone their SPC skills. The goal is to roll the training out by (date).

ABC Company Vision / Mission Statement

Vision: To be a recognized Performance Improvement Leader.
Mission: To ensure continuous individual and organizational performance improvement, supporting quality initiatives and corporate strategic goals.

ABC Company has initiated the eLT SPC project to support these aims.

ABC Company Criteria for Success

Desired finished course and organizational impact characteristics:

- Observable impact on job performance with evidence that trainees in the target audiences actually use SPC on the job to measure the consistency of processes (i.e., training that teaches SPC concepts and skills *and* motivates trainees to apply them on the job).
- High degree of support and buy-in by ABC Company stakeholder organizations for implementation of the eLT SPC in the learning environment leading to high usage of eLT SPC product (i.e., stakeholder representatives and organizations foster effective implementation, encourage audience members to complete the eLT SPC training, and support application of their SPC knowledge and skills to improve processes).
- eLT SPC should be a leap beyond the current standard of instructional effectiveness, creativity, and lasting impact that has been achieved by previous ABC Company eLT products.
- eLT SPC should be a worthy candidate for award recognition in multimedia training industry.

Desired characteristics of design and development process:

- Design and communication process that allows ABC Company to make informed choices about the impact of design decisions.
- Development and communication processes that are "agony free" (i.e., avoid negative surprises), enjoyable (i.e., including as many positive surprises as possible), and a general sense by ABC Company that its expectations have been met or exceeded.
- ABC Company should not have to catch major content errors or do significant editing to achieve desired level of clarity and fit for target audiences.
- ABC Company desires skill and knowledge transfer with regard to the SAM process and its methods for designing and developing memorable learning experiences.
- Achieve open, direct, and solution-focused communication so that problems are identified and resolved as soon as possible.
- Where possible, identify opportunities for ABC Company to improve its processes to simplify administration and record keeping.

Design and Development Process

The project will be using the SAM design and development process to create the eLT. This process is the successive approximation model of design and development.

Matrix

Content & Objectives x Treatment Matrix

The below matrix shows the initial identification of the eLT SPC content, its sequencing and the instructional treatments that can be successfully designed and developed to meet ABC Company's learning objectives within the given budget and schedule constraints and is based on what was learned during the information gathering and SAM cycles:

Focus Questions and Objectives	Instructional Treatments									
	Process Context (Dynamic)	Charts (Dynamic)	Classification	Question/Answer	Location/ Identification	Construction	Task Model	Tidbit	Demo/ Presentation	Resources /Tools
Module 1: UNDERSTANDING CURRENT PROCESS PERFORMANCE										
Lesson 1: Detection, Prevention and Improvement										
We're 100% inspecting already. Isn't that good enough?										
Identify characteristics of detection (inspection and sorting)			c			a				
Identify benefits and drawbacks of detection			c							
Can't I just use my experience to prevent problems?										
Identify characteristics of prevention: Recognize the importance of meeting specs			c							
Identify the effects of a typical prevention strategy: Recognize the effects of tampering		a		a						
Identify benefits and drawbacks of prevention			c							
Compare benefits and drawbacks of detection and prevention			c							

Focus Questions and Objectives	Instructional Treatments									
	Process Context (Dynamic)	Charts (Dynamic)	Classification	Question/Answer	Location/ Identification	Construction	Task Model	Tidbit	Demo/ Presentation	Resources /Tools
Lesson 2: Variation (Source and Distribution)										
Where does variation come from?										
Classify specific sources of variation according to the five main categories of variation sources: People Environment Equipment Materials Methods			a	d						
List the five main categories of variation sources			a	d						
How can I see how much variation I have?										
Given data, construct time order plots Recognize drawbacks of time order plots—What's the total spread of the data? Are there many points at the extremes? What portion? Where is the process centered? It's easier to get this information with a tally chart. Recognize that points vary even if nothing appears to be changing in the process		c, d		a						
Given a tally chart with a bell curve overlay, describe normal distribution in terms of average and spread		b, c, d		a						
Identify the effects of variation stack-up within part characteristics: Cancellation of sources Partial cancellation of sources Addition of sources		b, c, d		a	b					

Focus Questions and Objectives	Instructional Treatments									
	Process Context (Dynamic)	Charts (Dynamic)	Classification	Question/Answer	Location/ Identification	Construction	Task Model	Tidbit	Demo/ Presentation	Resources /Tools
When should I adjust my process to compensate for variation?										
Define control chart: Tracks data over time and establishes limits								a		
Observe sources of variation and their effects on time order plots		e								
Describe common cause variation and bounds (strong emphasis; use AIAG definitions)		e			a			a		
Describe special cause variation (strong emphasis; use AIAG definitions)	a	e						a		
Experiment with the effects of tampering by manipulating common and special variation causes and examining their effects on a tally chart	a	a		a						
Lesson 3: Definition of SPC										
OK, just what is SPC?										
Construct a diagram of the SPC process				b		a				
Describe each element of the SPC diagram				b		a				
Define SPC				b		a				
Module 2: APPLYING CONTROL CHARTS	Remainder of table is similar to above, but omitted to save space									
Module 3: USING SPC TO IMPROVE PROCESS										
Module 4: DEVELOPING SPC PLANS										
Module 5: CONSTRUCTING CONTROL CHARTS										
Module 6: INTEGRATING SPC METHODS										

Instructional Treatments

Following are descriptions of the contexts and instructional activities identified on the previous matrix.

Process Context (Dynamic):

a. Variation Viewer that allows learners to see and control special variation and view effects on chart.

Charts (Dynamic):

a. Tally chart (with bars and specs overlay) that responds dynamically to three or fewer learner controls (sliders) for special variation: X, XX, and XXX.

b. Normal curve (with spec limits) that responds to slider controls for location and spread and shows percent defective.

c. Tally chart—blank for learner construction. Data are generated according to parameters; learners plot points from generated data. System can automatically complete tally chart after learners successfully plot (n) points.

d. Chart—blank for learner plotting. Chart type is adjustable by author. Data are generated according to parameters; learners plot points from generated data. System can automatically complete chart after learners successfully plot (n) points.

e. Time order plot (plotted automatically) compresses into tally chart; then bell-shaped overlay is added.

f. Chart with generated data and boundaries/control limits that can be dragged up and down; chart type is adjustable by author.

g. Chart interpretation and investigation model: Chart type is adjustable by author (X-bar and R, Individuals and Moving Range, C, and P). Data and rules used to detect patterns are adjustable by author. Special causes are associated with one or more investigation tools.

Basic tools (available for all audiences):
- logs
- interviews with process participants
- possible tool = information extracted from SWI

Advanced tools:
- information extracted from sampling plan (could be extracted from Control Plan or header of control chart)
- previous control charts / logs
- information extracted from PFMEA

Learners drag sliders, drag circle/box, or click points to locate shift, trend, or point out-of-control. Learners examine process information tools to identify the associated cause. They collect evidence to support their claim.

Instructional Treatments (continued)

Classification:

a. Classification without all categories (no justification): Learners receive a series of items (one at a time) and one category for classification. If the item can be appropriately classified into the given category, learners select the category, and the next item in the list appears. If the item cannot be appropriately classified into the given category, learners click a button to indicate that another category is needed. The correct category appears, and learners select it. Two categories are now available as the next word in the list appears. If, at any time, learners classify an item into an incorrect category, the category disappears from the screen and does not reappear until learners receive an item that necessitates the category be reinstated ("Give me another category"). After incorrectly classifying an item, learners must continue to try to classify that item until they have located the appropriate category. Positive or negative feedback is provided after each classification attempt. Classification continues until learners have correctly classified the entire list.

b. Classification without all categories (with justification): Learners receive a series of items (one at a time) and one category for classification. If the item can be appropriately classified into the given category, learners select the category. They then answer a follow-up multiple-choice question about why the item belongs in the selected category. Positive or negative feedback is provided, and the next item in the list appears. If the item cannot be appropriately classified into the given category, learners click a button to indicate that another category is needed. The correct category appears, and learners select it. Two categories are now available as the next word in the list appears. If, at any time, learners classify an item into an incorrect category, the category disappears from the screen and does not re-appear until learners receive an item that necessitates the category be reinstated ("Give me another category"). After incorrectly classifying an item, learners must continue to try to classify that item until they have located the appropriate category. Positive or negative feedback is provided after each classification attempt. Classification continues until learners have correctly classified the entire list.

c. Classification with all categories (no justification): Learners receive a series of items and all available categories for classification. Learners select the appropriate category, and the next item appears. If learners incorrectly classify an item, they must continue to try to classify that item until they have located the appropriate category. Positive or negative feedback is provided after each classification attempt. Classification continues until learners have correctly classified the entire list.

Instructional Treatments (continued)	**Question and Answer:**

Question and Answer:

a. Multiple choices (one correct answer): Learners read/hear stem of question and lettered answers. Learners select correct answer. Positive or negative feedback is provided.

b. Multiple choices (one correct answer)—with justification follow-up: Learners read/hear stem of question and lettered answers. Learners select correct answer. Each multiple-choice question is followed by a custom multiple-choice question to determine why learners answered either correctly or incorrectly.

c. True and False with multiple-choice follow-up.

d. Text entry.

Location/Identification:

a. Learners drag markers to pinpoint an area on a graphic or chart.

b. Learners click to pinpoint an area on a graphic or chart.

Construction:

a. Learners drag elements of a graphic into place; custom feedback is provided for each positive/negative attempt. Construction continues until learners successfully place each element.

Remainder of instructional treatments is similar to above, but omitted to save space.

Managing Scope

Defined Scope

ABC Company has described the scope of the project in general terms, but the final scope cannot yet be defined fully. The following key deliverables will need to be prepared and approved by ABC Company to complete the scope definition:

- target performance outcomes
- content scope and objectives by treatment matrix
- design proof

Scope Change Management

After the scope has been defined and approved, proposed changes (e.g. design, quantity of content, or schedule) that may affect the planned budget or schedule will be subject to the following change management procedures:

- If requested changes affect approved designs or completed work, the cost and schedule implications of the changes will be determined, discussed, and approved before they are implemented.
- Requested changes that do not impact the budget or schedule will be described in writing and approved before they are implemented.
- Other requested changes that impact the budget or schedule, such as added content, will require analysis, a written impact statement, and approval. The cost of conducting the analysis and preparing the impact statement will be provided and need approval before the analysis begins.

Quality

User Testing Plan

User testing is the only reliable method of determining the proposed learning solution's integrity and impact.

When in the development process:

- early prototypes
- design proof
- alpha release
- beta release

Guidelines for whom to involve:

- The best users to involve in user testing include people from the target population, both those who have not been trained and those who have been trained recently.

Quality Assurance/ Quality Compliance

Quality Assurance/Quality Compliance (QA/QC) is the use of procedures that are important throughout the process to assure attention to and achievement of quality is happening. The QA resources on the project will assume the role of user advocate, examining all areas of the solution for appropriateness, completion, and effectiveness. The specific types of testing conducted on this project will be:

Integration testing. This type of testing evaluates the interaction between combined components in a learning solution. Typically, developers and/or QA/QC team members conduct this test iteratively during the coding of new or the addition of reusable learning objects as they are integrated into a course.

Usability testing. This type of testing evaluates the usability of a learning solution and/or its components. Usability denotes a learning solution or component's ease of use, intuitiveness, performance, and user-friendliness.

Editorial testing/editing. This type of testing focuses on grammar, spelling, and other editorial issues. The editing ideally will take place at a point in which the content is solid and has client sign-off.

Functional testing. This type of testing evaluates adherence to the intended design, functionality, usability, external links, and overall performance of the complete, integrated learning solution.

Scope of Quality Assurance

To most effectively address the widest range of testing coverage, the following table illustrates the relationships among the different types of QA testing, participants in these testing types, and the development phase in which these testing types take place:

Type of Testing	Development Phase
Integration Testing	Design Proof
Usability Testing	Design Proof
Editorial Testing/ Editing	Alpha
Functional Testing	Alpha

Projected Milestones & Deliverables

Additional information regarding subject matter expert (SME) availability and user interview schedules will play a key role in scheduling.

Below please find a list of the interim and final deliverables for the project, brief descriptions of each task, and an estimated timeline.

- All deliverable dates are considered to be close of business. ABC Company is able to review the deliverable by the start of the next business day.
- All deliverables will be posted on the project webpage, including builds, documents, and media comps.

Schedule

Deliverable	Description	Process to Create	Date for Delivery for Approval
1. Project Management Plan	Summarizes the project as initially understood. Establishes the framework for managing project.	Prepare draft for discussion. Obtain approval.	date
2. Statement of Business Need	Summarizes problems and opportunities addressed by this project from perspective of represented stakeholder organizations.	Interview SMEs during analysis meetings. Prepare draft statement for review and comment. Submit for approval.	date
3. Delivery Platform	Defines hardware and software characteristics of delivery workstations and networks. Defines testing procedures to assure eLT SPC operates without error and with adequate performance for defined platform(s).	Interview for general parameters, benefits and trade-offs. Conduct internal research and establish minimum platform. Prepare draft statement for review. Refine and submit for approval.	date
4. Learning Environment	Describes processes by which end users are invited/assigned to enroll in eLT CBT and outlines likely conditions in which eLT CBT may be used.	Interview SMEs during analysis meetings. Prepare draft statement for review and comment. Submit for approval.	date
5. Assessment/Tracking Plan	Defines the role of testing / learner assessment. Defines data to be tracked and procedures for data collection and analysis.	Interview HR. Prepare draft statement for review and comment. Submit for approval.	date
6. Audience Characteristics	Defines audience(s) by job function. For each audience, identifies demographic characteristics / motivational factors that may constrain or guide design. Also identifies assumed prerequisite knowledge and skills.	Interview HR, project sponsor, and managers. Prepare draft statement for review and comment. Submit for approval.	date

Deliverable	Description	Process to Create	Date for Delivery for Approval
7. Target Performance Outcomes	For each audience, defines target performance outcomes and related learning objectives in measurable terms.	Interview HR, project sponsor, and managers. Prepare draft statement for review and comment. Submit for approval.	date
8. Skills Hierarchy/Content Scope	For each audience, determines range and depth of content coverage and skills to be taught.	Interview HR, performance managers, and SMEs. Prepare draft statement for review and comment. Submit for approval.	date
9. Objectives x Treatments Matrix	Shows how learning activities and objectives are related (i.e., which learning activities address specific objectives).	Prepare draft statement for review and comment. Submit for approval.	date
10. Content Preparation Plan	Defines style and usage guidelines for text including approved technical terminology. Defines file formats and other technical standards for images, audio, video, animation, drawings, illustrations, etc. Establishes structures and formats for instructional narrative scripts, video scripts, etc. as used in specific interaction formats. Establishes guidelines for preparing case studies and scenarios, test questions, simulation exercises, etc. Describes procedures for content preparation, editing, and approvals.	Collect sources of text style and usage guidelines and approved technical terminology. Identify standards for media and procedures for working with video supplier. Determine formats for preparing scenarios, case studies, etc. to assure ease of review by internal SMEs. Prepare draft statement for review and comment. Submit for approval.	date
11. Prototypes of All Design Components (multiple iterations)	Interactive treatments for teaching objectives of representative samples of content. Iterative design proceeds through a sequence of design/prototyping/evaluation cycles in which successively more comprehensive samples of content are addressed until all core interactions have been planned. Multiple cycles of iterative design allow the team to collaborate in seeking effective design solutions for each content/skill type for each audience. Prototypes in early cycles address small but representative sets of content and use rudimentary levels of media and program logic. Some design ideas are accepted for further refinement while others may be rejected or redirected. Later cycles include broader samples of content treated in more depth with richer media and/or more robust logic. Prototyping continues until all planned content types and treatments have been adequately explored.	Following the information gathering phase and general approval of analysis findings (as summarized in deliverables 2 – 8), lead a series of rapid collaborative prototyping sessions (Savvy Start). Develop a series of prototypes in which the focus of prototyping and evaluation shifts progressively through the following sequence: Content Revised Content Navigation & Graphic Design Revised Navigation & Graphic Design Interactivity I Interactivity II Content & Interactivity Digital Assets & Interactivity Contingency (if additional cycles are needed to complete goals of earlier cycles).	The first sessions in this series are scheduled for *date* (following stakeholder review, refinement, and approval of information-gathering findings). Prototyping will continue, as needed, until all planned content types and treatments have been adequately explored.

Deliverable	Description	Process to Create	Date for Delivery for Approval
12. User Testing	User testing is the only reliable method of determining the proposed learning solutions integrity and impact.	Identify user testing candidates from the target audience (trained and not trained). Schedule and hold user testing sessions. Submit findings for review and discussion.	date
13. Design Proof	A blueprint of the project. Design proofs will include functional prototypes and may contain documentation, existing interactions, flow charts, class diagrams, and any other necessary information to design the application as a whole.	Consolidate findings from information gathering, Savvy Start, project planning, and additional design cycles into the design proof. Submit for approval.	date
14. Content Grids/Scripts/ Media Specifications	Complete narratives, scripts, and media specifications.	Propose formats, standards for content narratives, media scripts and specifications in Content Preparation Plan. SMEs identify case studies and examples as outlined in the design proof and objectives x treatments matrix. Edit and/or write content narratives, media scripts and specifications applying standards and guidelines established in the Content Preparation Plan. Submit content narratives, media scripts and specifications for approval.	Specific items and their scheduled delivery will be identified in the schedule for production cycles.
15. Media Assets	Illustrations, photos, audio, video, and animations.	Prepare content-specific graphics, charts, graphs, and animations. Produce audio using approved voice talent. Produce and edit video using approved on-camera and voice talent. Submit media assets as they are completed for review and approval.	Specific items and scheduled delivery will be identified in the schedule for production cycles.
16. Learning Modules	Usable learning materials. As content elements are prepared and approved, they will be integrated into the program to create the learning activities/ modules planned for the eLT SPC.	Integrate content, media, and interactive elements into the models and navigation structures created during alpha production cycles. Conduct planned internal QA procedures. Submit developed learning modules for approval.	date range
17. Alpha Release	Completed and functional product with faults identified from QA process but not all remedied.	Integrate all developed learning modules into a complete product. Submit for review and user testing.	date
18. Beta Release	Completed corrections identified in testing, if any.	Conduct further beta testing as needed. Submit for acceptance.	date
19. Gold Release	Completed modifications, if any are required.	Submit for final acceptance.	date

Roles & Responsibilities

Effective resource planning is a complex process of both short- and long-term planning. The table below lists general project responsibilities for the ABC Company stakeholders and business sponsors and the project development team:

Sponsor

1. Work with development team to define, organize, collect and refine of all content, including text, graphics, audio, etc.

2. Act as the intermediary between the users and other stakeholders, assisting in data collection and gathering feedback about prototypes.

3. Assist in the creation of prototypes through participation in analysis and design.

4. Provide timely access to ABC Company's subject matter experts for purposes of clarifying content and reviewing deliverables.

5. Produce video and audio for inclusion in application.

6. Conduct quality compliance testing on deliverables and assist with pilot group testing.

7. Provide timely feedback (i.e., modification, acceptance or rejection) on all project deliverables including feedback from stakeholders and business sponsors.

Development Team

1. Use SAM for project design, development and management.

2. Work with the sponsor to organize and define content for the application.

3. Retain sources of subject matter expertise.

4. Create prototypes through iterative analysis and design.

5. Produce the application (authoring, programming, graphic creation, etc.).

6. Incorporate quality assurance into the design and development process, perform quality compliance testing on all deliverables and assist with user group testing.

7. Make minor content changes/corrections and provide support for a period of 180 days following delivery and acceptance of the final training course.

8. Manage all project-related activities.

Project Sponsor

Role/Individual	Project Responsibilities
Business Sponsor **Jerry Jackson** Exec VP of Operations	• Review key project deliverables during project. • Approve final training course.
Key Stakeholder **Jennifer Hughes** VP of Quality Assurance	• Review key project deliverables during project. • Approve final training course.
Project Lead **John Smith**	• Assure effective communication among all parties. • Coordinate all ABC Company internal meetings. • Manage ABC Company project schedule to planned milestones. • Coordinate all approvals including those of stakeholders and business sponsors. • Conduct project review meetings. • Participate in project planning processes, task assignments, and criteria for milestone completion. • Grant final approval of all milestones. • Gain internal ABC Company consensus on all subject matter and multimedia deliverables. • Communicate project status internally and externally. • Assist and participate in analysis and design activities. • Assist in preparing content. • Coordinate review of all deliverables by ABC Company project team and subject matter experts. • Assure coordination of all activities relating to project. • Assure project success.
Lead Subject Matter Expert **Joe Jones**	• Assist and participate in analysis and design activities. • Help establish learning and performance objectives. • Help plan case studies and examples. • Assist in preparing content for use in the course. • Review deliverables assigned for review by ABC Company Project Lead.
Computer and Network Liaison **Tina Jackson**	• Assist and participate in design activities. • Review developed content for inconsistencies and technical errors. • Be source for database and computer questions. • Coordinate all reviews and approvals of IT department.
Instructor **Bill Apple**	• Assist and participate in design activities. • Review developed content for inconsistencies and technical errors. • IT liaison.

If changes to assignments or additional ABC Company participants are identified, the ABC Company Project Lead will discuss the changes/additions with the development team so the impact on the project schedule can be determined.

Development Team

Role/Individual	Project Responsibilities
Project Executive **Mary Jefferson**	• Assure continuous and effective communication among all parties. • Assure ABC Company satisfaction with process and deliverables. • Manage Change Order process.
Senior Producer **Jane Thomas**	• Plan schedule; manage planned milestones. • Plan budget; manage budget. • Monitor ABC Company satisfaction with process and deliverables. • Plan processes, task assignments, and criteria for milestone completion. • Plan and manage assignments of project team and consultant resources for analysis, design, production, and evaluation activities. • Write/edit deliverable reports. • Manage QA/QC processes for deliverables. • Manage ABC Company approvals of deliverables. • Communicate project status to team and to ABC Company. • Conduct assigned technical activities in analysis, design, production, and evaluation.
Instructional Strategist **Ted Simpson**	• Analyze the project's instructional strategy and make recommendations. • Help prepare the instructional components. • Lead and assist in the design and development of prototypes during design phase. • Provide reviews, attend meetings, and assist with project redesigns throughout the life of the project.
Associate Producer/ Content Writer **Sharilyn Francis**	• Prepare meeting summaries, project management reports, document processes, and provide other administrative support, as assigned. • Assist in briefing supplemental team members. • Assist in preparing Content Preparation Plan. • Gather/edit content from ABC Company and consultant SMEs. • Write audio/video scripts, as needed. • Write reference/instructional text, as needed. • Write and lay out user's manual, if included in design. • Edit content prepared by other team members and consultant SMEs. • Assist in assuring quality of deliverables. • Conduct other assigned technical activities in analysis, design, production, and evaluation.

Development Team (continued)

Role/Individual	Project Responsibilities
Lead Interactivity Engineer **Bob Brown**	• Share in planning processes and criteria for milestone completion. • Participate in core analysis and design activities. • Create functional prototypes. • Engineer navigation shell and models, including methods for managing data sets, simulation environments for exploring relationships among production parameters and measured attributes, etc. • Brief/train supplemental interactivity engineers/interactivity developers, as needed. • Develop interactive content during production, as needed. • Conduct other analysis, design, production, and evaluation activities as assigned.
Consulting Subject Matter Expert **David Luce, PhD**	• Assist in analysis and design activities as assigned. • Help establish learning and performance objectives. • Provide subject matter understanding to development team. • Help plan case studies and examples. • Assist in preparing Content Preparation Plan. • Prepare content narratives, data sets, etc. for assigned topics/activities per design summary and Content Preparation Plan. • Review developed content (e.g., author ready narratives, storyboards, scripts, completed modules, etc.) for content accuracy and effectiveness with audience.
Interactivity Developer **Mike Saunders**	• Write and test programming code. • Support the lead interactivity engineer throughout the project to develop the courseware. • Troubleshoot and research technical issues.
Media Artist **Martha Noonen**	• Design and create media prototypes. • Create media assets for task production. • Modify the graphics related to the navigation interface • Consult regarding screen design and information management of screens.
Quality Compliance **Michelle Cook**	• Manage and direct all quality compliance testing.

If changes to assignments or additional team participants are identified, the senior producer will discuss the changes or additions with the ABC Company Project Lead so that the impact on the project schedule can be determined.

Decision Making

Approval

Who Has *Sign-Off* Authority On...?	Name of Decision Maker	Decision Is Binding? (Yes or No)
Interface/Look and feel	John Smith	Yes
Technical issues	John Smith	Yes
Budget/Schedule	John Smith	Yes
Content/Subject matter	John Smith	Yes
Instructional design	John Smith	Yes
Acceptance review	John Smith	Yes

Communications Plan and Issue Resolution

Primary Contact Responsibility

The ABC Project Lead and Development Team Senior Producer listed above will be responsible for communicating significant events and activity to members of their organizations as necessary. Although a free flow of communication is valuable, primary contacts should always be kept informed.

Although most communication will occur in meetings and teleconferences, use of email and written summaries of verbal correspondence will also be encouraged in order to provide a record of decisions, issues, solutions, and project status.

Project Status

Project status will be communicated to the ABC Project Lead by the following means:

- Starting after acceptance of the Project Management Plan, a bi-weekly Project Status Report will be prepared and delivered to the ABC Project Lead via email. This report will provide an overview of project status, schedule status of the deliverables for the project, listing of milestones in the upcoming weeks, and identification/status update of issues that have arisen and the actions to fix the issues.
- Throughout the project, the ABC Project Lead will be apprised of the status of project activities through regular verbal and email communications.

Email Protocol	• Although email may be used to communicate decisions, as a general rule, "official" decisions that could impact design, schedule or scope will not be made via email only, but also communicated verbally. • Material project management decisions will be captured in an updated Project Management Plan. Design or technical decisions will be reflected in the Design Proof.
Course Comments & Fixes	• Prototype comments will be gathered in an electronic document, organized by priority. • All requested changes after alpha build will be logged and tracked electronically.
Meeting Planning	Non-recurring meeting planning will be initiated via email between ABC Project Lead and Development Team Senior Producer to determine scheduling availability. Follow-up phone call(s) as necessary.
Best Practices	• For situations requiring immediate attention, an email will be sent that clearly explains the situation followed-up by a phone call. • Team members' time out of the office and/or on vacation will be noted and communicated as far in advance as possible throughout the life of the project. • Project managers will always be looking two weeks forward and make special note of upcoming events within the next two-week period.
File Transfer	ABC Company will provide access to its SharePoint site as well as log-in(s) and password(s). This can be used for larger files that are not considered official deliverables (e.g., background research files, content documents, resources, images, etc.). Smaller files will be zipped and sent as email attachments.

Project Webpage

All deliverables will be made available via a project webpage with the exception of the final deliverables of source content and gold master for LMS implementation. ABC Company's user ID and password will be provided via a secure email.

The project webpage will display deliverables for both builds and documents, as well reflect changes to either of the above.

- When an update has been made to a previous deliverable (for example, to the Project Management Plan), a new link will be shown with the new date, along with notes which provide a brief overview of what has changed.
- The above process will help provide a history trail of the entire project in terms of prototypes, media, functional builds, project plans, design, and development documents.

Issue Resolution

Issues will be communicated and resolved by the following means:

- Upon identification of an issue, the ABC Project Lead or Senior Project Producer will communicate the existence of the issue via email or telephone and proposed actions for solving it.
- The teams will work diligently to determine a mutually agreed-upon action or actions to solve the issue.
- If the ABC Project Lead and Senior Project Producer are unable to reach a mutually agreed-upon solution, the following individuals will review the issues and determine the resolution:
  - ABC Company: Jennifer Hughes
  - Development Team: Mary Jefferson

Project Risks

No project is without risk. Below are some identified risks and initial strategies to mitigate them.

Risk	Possible Impact	Likelihood	Action Steps to Minimize Risk
Inadequate communication and consensus among stakeholders	Difficult to schedule consistent participation. Difficult/time consuming to achieve consensus. Could delay reviews and approvals.	Medium to high	Work at outset to define expectations for nature and timing of participation. Seek stakeholder buy-in to project's product and process goals. Seek to establish rapport and establish clear and open communication. ABC Project Lead accepts responsibility of consolidating stakeholder input and, where necessary, of making decisions on behalf of stakeholders. ABC Project Lead is available, as needed, for project (i.e., essentially full time).
Delays in reviews and approval of deliverables, prototypes, and requests for guidance	Inefficient use of resources. Delay of dependent activities.	Medium	Clear communication about expected timeframe for reviews and/or decisions. ABC Project Lead to manage schedule for internal reviews. ABC Company to promote enthusiasm and responsiveness among participating reviewers.
Internal SMEs' conflicting biases about design parameters that are not easily resolved. Internal SMEs' biases that are not expressed until late in the project	Design process and eventual design could be too tightly or prematurely constrained. Could slow design process or limit potential for impact.	Medium to high	Set expectations for open communication and collaborative problem solving (vs. adopting pre-established mindsets). Consider broad range of opinions and options in working toward a widely supported solution. Seek confirmation of design ideas through user testing.
Audience variation (i.e., factory line manufacturing employees appear to be significantly different from other audiences and may have significant within-group variation)	Course may not fit specific audience(s) well. Needed training may not be accessible for a portion of the audience (limiting potential impact on performance). Difficult to manage scope. Difficult to manage logistics for user testing.	High	Establish prerequisites such that constraints of one audience don't reduce effectiveness for other audiences. Consider use of audience-specific modules/ treatments. Consider development of separate eLT SPC products.
Insufficient access to audiences for testing	Could limit ability to identify and match real needs of audiences. Complex logistics could limit number or timeliness of usability trials.	Low	ABC Company enlists support of stakeholder representatives to identify and prepare participants for usability testing and small group trials. ABC Company plans and manages logistics, as required.

Risk	Possible Impact	Likelihood	Action Steps to Minimize Risk
Audience resistance (i.e., some trainees may resist learning or may acquire knowledge and skills but choose not to apply them –"know how but won't")	Limit impact on performance. Limit ability to satisfy stated business need.	Medium	Identify effective motivational "hooks" for each audience. Anticipate barriers to application of trained skills in work environment. Consider management incentives program to encourage support. Consider an implementation training project to assist managers to become effective change agents for implementation of SPC .
Differences between academic and job environments (real or perceived barriers to implementation)	Training perceived as irrelevant. Training perceived as inconsistent with current practices.	Medium	Choose realistic examples. Use divergent examples to promote generalization of concepts. Address importance of sample planning, accurate measurement. Illustrate effects of ill-considered shortcuts, sloppiness, etc. on quality of data and value of SPC as a tool.
Inadequate support for implementation of training in learning environment	Training does not reach intended audiences. Trainees are de-motivated from learning.	Medium	ABC Company to work with stakeholder representatives to plan effective implementation of training.
Constraints on application of SPC in performance environment (i.e., constraints/biases limiting transfer of training to job)	Limit impact on performance.	Medium	ABC Company enlists support of stakeholder representatives to identify constraints/ opportunities on implementation of SPC in work environment. ABC Company plans demonstrations of eLT SPC to key personnel within plants and other end-user organizations.

CHAPTER 13

Additional Design

Unless the project is small or a small set of instructional designs covers all types and instances of content, the Savvy Start does not complete all the design work necessary. There are probably objectives not yet defined and written. The content has not yet been put in final sequence if in any sequence at all. Homework, projects, navigation, aids, and many other components may not have been given much attention.

COMPLETING THE DESIGN
It isn't the purpose of the Savvy Start to create all the content or even approach final form. Text, graphics, and other preparations have yet to be done, but this work is part of iterative development yet to come. At this point we look to finishing up the design work.

Iterations Continue
The process of additional design is not a new process. The same process used for the Savvy Start continues with iterations of design, prototyping, and evaluation.

Special-Purpose Prototypes
It is also in this phase of the process when special-purpose prototypes are created. These prototypes may take more time and effort than the Savvy Start permits (which is in part why they are not done then) and deal with issues that require special expertise.

Frequently needed special-purpose prototypes include:

- **Look-and-feel**—This type of prototype focuses on layout and style for print materials, projected materials, and electronic devices, including division of screen areas, color, text fonts, and effects such as drop shadows (additionally for e-learning, use of mouse gestures, touch input, etc.).
- **Media**—The media prototype demonstrates the use of photography, audio recordings, 3D illustration, video, and so on.
- **Role-playing**—Many topics lend themselves well to role-playing, but constructing successful role-playing events is not easy. Role-playing events need to be tested by creating prototype challenges and playing them out.
- **Navigation**—This type of prototype should demonstrate options learners will have to move from activity to activity, to bookmark places to return to, and to access reference material and services such as glossary, notebook, and calculator.
- **Network/LMS integration**—When forms of electronic delivery are in play, it's important not to rely on assumptions of what the network can and will do to support a project. It's smart to build a prototype at this point to test services and interfaces to avoid surprises perhaps no one suspects.

Special-purpose prototypes can be invaluable in finalizing design. The alternative approach of writing specifications, finalizing them, and getting approvals sounds expedient, but without prototypes, such methods tend to result in rework after development. In total, any process without prototypes is likely to be longer or result in inferior products.

It's Still Just Three Iterations

Three iterations of a prototype are usually about right to make sure neither too much nor too little attention goes into the design. After three iterations the return on time and effort decreases significantly.

PART III

Iterative Development Phase

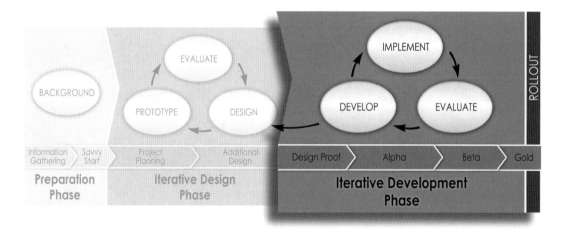

The three-step iterative approach continues in the development phase of SAM2, which differs from SAM1 by separating development cycles from design cycles rather than interleaving them. While we prefer tightly coupling design and development and evolving prototypes into final products, many practical necessities are accommodated by separating them.

CHAPTER 14

Creating the Design Proof

When the objectives x treatments matrix is completed, the development team can begin its work to build the final product. Of note is that the process doesn't change radically from earlier phases and tasks. Quite the contrary, it continues almost unchanged.

Iterations continue, but now the work builds on accepted and approved designs. Instead of designing learning events, the iterative cycles create and implement content in the framework provided by the designs. Instead of disposable prototypes, iterations produce a series of approximations to the final product: design proof, alpha release, beta release, and finally the final or "gold" release. Iteration One produces the design proof. It is a final check on the design direction before undertaking development of all content in

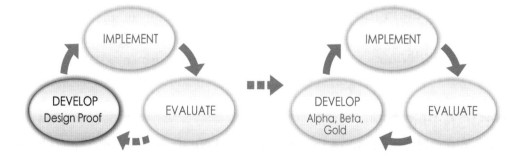

subsequent iterations. Iteration Two produces the alpha release candidate, and Iteration Three produces the beta release candidate. If the beta release has no unacceptable flaws, it becomes the final product. If it has problems, another beta release is produced. The process continues until a beta release is accepted for rollout—the gold release.

AVOIDING THE BEST IDEA

It would make everything so much easier if all the best ideas surfaced at the start of a project. Unfortunately, great ideas are unruly and disobedient. They fail to arrive when beckoned, vanish just when you need them most, and speak up when you wish they'd be silent. Everybody likes a good idea, but there are times when they're just short of painful. A lot of work has been done and you're almost finished, and then… and then, the idea pounces. *Here's what we really should have done!* Oh, no.

There's a reason good ideas arrive late: They're predicated on and born of all the foundational thinking that's been done to define the questions. *What really needs to be done? What do learners really need to do? How can we best motivate learning?* Reviewing candidate solutions would seem to focus one on detailed attributes of the solutions, and it does, but it also focuses attention on the problem and ultimately reveals a better understanding of it. As solutions become more complete, they reveal the more hidden nuances of the problem and additional needs. And that's when the *best* solution occurs. Right?

No.

It seems there's *always* a better solution lying in wait. Implement that best solution and just as it's about nailed, *You know what? Here's what we* really *should do!*

It's important not only for sanity, but also for delivering on time and budget, to avoid thinking there's a perfect solution in reach. One of those unruly, disobedient great ideas is *always* lying in wait. *Always.* The best advice: Follow the successive approximation process, iterate a controlled number of times, and produce a successful product. After some time in the field, it may be appropriate to iterate a bit more. That can be done with the benefit of performance data and feedback. But trying for perfection is always a doomed agenda.

> **Better ideas fail to arrive when beckoned, vanish just when you need them most, and speak up when you wish they'd be silent.**

THE DESIGN PROOF

The design proof is the output of the first development cycle. It's something of a bridge between design and development. Remember that SAM2, the process we're detailing here, is for larger projects where there's a need to more formally separate design and development. In SAM1 we continue to keep design and development interleaved until a final product emerges.

The design proof begins the iterative development cycle and offers a critical opportunity to view all the designed components of the instructional product integrated with each other. This is the time to confirm design decisions. Most specifically, this is the time to check whether expectations are being met, that the approach will work as a whole, and if there are any problems with the design.

Important: Confirmation is accomplished with an intentionally incomplete version that brings all pieces of the design together for the first time. Content and media development are limited so that minimal effort will be required for a change of direction, if necessary, but representative media are finally in place and very much open for assessment.

The design proof contains the following:
- All structural components are present and functional, including at least one instructional event of every type designed for the product.
- Sample graphics and other media are included in final resolution, but placeholders remain for the majority of instances.
- Sample content is included for each major content area and is complete for at least one instance of each different instructional treatment. Otherwise, placeholders will be used.
- Navigation and interactivity structures collect sample performance data sufficient to test data collection and interconnectivity to external data files and LMS as appropriate.
- Instructor's Guide and notes, as appropriate, allow an instructor not part of the design and development team to actually conduct a class, section, or instructional event.

Less Is Faster

While it's very important to confirm the effectiveness of the design, spending too much time on the design proof can be counterproductive. Sample interactions should effectively demonstrate a complete learning activity, but many components can be mockups, simulated, or duplicated to reduce development time needed for proofing the design. Developers need to make a judgment call on what items are critical to effectively demonstrate each design feature or activity. But at least one finished component of every type intended to be used should be included.

For example, in e-learning, the code to create the logic behind an elaborate branching learning event requires considerable development time. However, sufficient effect of this activity can easily be revealed with some of the learner's choices inactive. It is more important for evaluators to see the flow of the activity, rather than every path that will be available in the final product.

The design proof is the time to pause and look at the course as a whole. This is a major transitional step between the initial design and the alpha release. It's likely that when everything comes together as it does in the design proof, it will invite some redesign. This is expected and should not be considered a fault of the design. Until all components are present and integrated, the learner's experience could only be imagined. When it becomes real, some problems and some opportunities are very likely to emerge. Perhaps a small change here or there will make a powerful learning experience come to life that was otherwise just under the surface.

Iteration in SAM, including even the development phase, makes discovering problems and opportunities happen as early as possible. Such discovery is invaluable, but it also carries the risk of being in revision mode perpetually.

Changes should definitely be made where problems exist and affordable opportunities are discovered, but the temptation to make radical revisions usually must be resisted. This is not just because of time and budget limitations—although those constraints may well be enough to prohibit major changes—but realizing that if major rework is allowed this time, it will be just as attractive again in the next round. It's almost always better to get a product in use, gain feedback, and *then* consider further refinements.

WRITING COURSE CONTENT

Design prototypes create a broad foundation on which to begin writing the course content. Even though we hope some exciting learning events have been designed, the course content— more than the number or type of events—will prove to be the most challenging work. Except for small courses, content development requires a structured and systematic approach.

At the start of the development cycles, the expected content is typically conveyed in a variety of ways, including elements of the prototypes, outlines, bulleted lists, references to documents, videos, and so on. The development team must now begin assembling or creating text, graphics, audio, video, and whatever other content is required.

The process of creating course content begins with the development of content grids— documents used to structure the context, challenges, activities, and feedback. The grids provide a method for writing, reviewing, and revising content. There will be a content grid for each learning event or each interaction. Figure 14-1 provides a content grid template.

Figure 14-1. Content Grid Template

Objective: [state objective]			
Context	[Describe situation]		
Challenge	[Describe what learner needs to accomplish]		
Activity	[Describe how learner will indicate what he or she observes or wants to do]		
Feedback	**Actions**	**Consequences**	**Judgments (if any)**
	[Describe actions learners might take, making a separate row for each]	[Describe consequence of taking this action]	[Describe judgment to be given and score change]
		[Describe consequence of not taking this action]	[Describe judgment to be given and score change]
[List next events and conditions for branching to each]			

To populate the grids for each topic and learning event, the team writes questions for the subject matter experts so they can provide the specific information needed. For example, if a learning event targets effective conversations between salespeople and customers, some content-gathering questions might be:

- What are the methods you want your salespeople to use when communicating with customers?
- What are some exemplary conversations salespeople might have with customers?
- What are the most common complaints of customers?
- What are the appropriate responses for each customer complaint?
- What mistakes do salespeople make in responding to each customer complaint?
- What are the likely outcomes of each mistake?
- Can mistakes be corrected? If so, how?
- What options do salespeople have to address customer issues?
- How do salespeople currently address customer complaints?
- What information or resources can salespeople access?

Identifying what salespeople and customers discuss, how they communicate, appropriate communication strategies, and resources available to salespeople, provides a realistic launch point for writing course content. Figure 14-2 shows an example content grid.

Figure 14-2. Example Content Grid: Identifying Road Construction Safety Hazards

Identifying Safety Hazards — Part I			
Context	*Scene Description: Highway lane painting containing hazardous and non-hazardous elements as described below.*		
	As a team leader, you are held accountable for the safety of your crew. When you arrive on a worksite, the very first thing you should do is quickly and thoroughly look around to identify, and correct, any areas where there is potential for danger.		
Challenge	In this activity, you will browse a worksite and identify potential safety hazards within 20 seconds.		
Activity	Using your mouse, click the people or items that present a safety hazard. Think you're up for the challenge? Let's get started!		
Feedback	**Actions: Correct/ Preferred**	**Consequences**	**Judgments (if any)**
	Click: Person wearing proper shoes bending over to pick up a cardboard box.	Safety warning triangle appears over box.	
		If not clicked: Person has an expletive (#$!) talk bubble come from his mouth and has his hand on his back.	
	Click: Truck backing up with a person standing behind it.	Safety warning triangle appears over person.	
		If not clicked: Person gets toes run over and shouts in agony.	

Feedback (continued)	Click: Lane closure with flaggers in the middle.	Safety warning triangle appears over the flaggers.	
		If not clicked: Flaggers nearly get struck by fast moving car as horn blares.	
	Click DONE button with all hazard(s) identified.	All warning triangle(s) blink.	"Well done. Remember, when you arrive on a worksite you need to quickly and thoroughly scan the scene for any potential hazards."
	Actions: Incorrect	**Consequences**	**Judgments (if any)**
	Click: People wearing appropriate gear riding the lane painting truck.	Team members stand looking angrily at their watch because they had to stop work for no reason.	"It is important to be safe, but remember that work still needs to get done."
	Click: Pedestrians walking across the street in a cross walk.	Pedestrians are all huddled waiting to cross the street and getting angry that they are not able to cross.	"While safety is paramount, it's important not to impede the public unnecessarily."
	Click DONE button with missed hazard(s).	Blinking warning triangle(s) appear over missed hazard(s).	"Uh-oh, looks like you missed something. Remember, when you arrive on a worksite you need to quickly and thoroughly scan the scene for any potential hazards."
Move learner on to Part II.			

Figure 14-3. e-Learning Produced From Content Grid in Figure 14-2

The content grid example shown in Figure 14-2 resulted in an interactive screen shown here in Figure 14-3. You can play much of the interactivity in your head by looking at this screen capture and reading through the content grid.

CHAPTER 15

Iterative Evaluation

Reviews of design prototypes have been focused on validating whether proposed learning events appropriately address the performance objectives, all content areas are being covered, and the interface is appropriate and effective. Those reviews were largely unstructured and general because the criteria, themselves, were fluid and up for reconsideration as necessary.

Evaluating the design proof is the first structured review of the emerging product. The structure helps keep focus on the issues relevant at this stage. For example, the design proof review should not focus on the completeness of content elements or interactive details, but rather on whether the course structure makes sense, whether challenges and activities are effective, and whether the key content areas are addressed.

The list of evaluation questions in Figure 15-1 offers guidelines for reviewing an e-learning design proof.

Figure 15-1. Design Proof Evaluation Checklist for e-Learning Projects

Navigation	☐ Is the navigation compliant with the organization's standards or consistent with other applications in use? ☐ Are the navigational elements recognizable and understandable? ☐ Are universally accepted conventions being used where appropriate? ☐ Does the menu effectively convey the course structure and content? ☐ Does the navigation provide access to required parts of the course with appropriate effort? ☐ If there are course resources, can the learner access them from everywhere they might be useful? ☐ Is it always clear to learners where they are within the application, how much they've learned, and how much remains? ☐ Can learners browse to look ahead or to review previous interactions? ☐ Are quit and resume functions working properly and available everywhere they should be? ☐ Are NEXT and BACK buttons working properly and available everywhere they should be? ☐ Are there "dead-ends"? (If so, make a note and describe them on a separate sheet.) ☐ Are any helpful navigational functions missing? (If so, make a note and describe them on a separate sheet.)
Media	☐ Are the representational media appealing and of appropriate quality? ☐ Are the representational media appropriate for this content and audience? ☐ Are media consistent with the organization's image and branding? ☐ Are media in compliance with the organization's style guide and media standards? ☐ Are sound effects helpful, consistent, and appropriate? ☐ Are any media not being displayed or presenting too slowly? ☐ Are media synchronized with each other on playback? ☐ Are media elements, including text, externalized for simplified maintenance or localization? ☐ Is display space allowed for future language translation and cultural adaptation?

Interaction	☐ Is it always clear what options the learner has? ☐ Do learners know what they are supposed to do and how to respond? ☐ Do the interactions work properly and respond promptly? ☐ Are the interactions relevant? ☐ Are the interactions engaging? ☐ Can users detect and correct their own errors before they are judged? ☐ Are the learning activities meaningful? ☐ Are the learning activities appropriately challenging? ☐ Are the learning activities memorable? ☐ Are the learning activities motivational? ☐ How does interacting with the course make learners feel? (Are the emotional reactions appropriate and helpful?)
Content	☐ Does the content address targeted behaviors effectively? ☐ Are scenarios relevant and appropriate to learners and the learning objectives? ☐ Is content worded correctly and readable at an appropriate level? ☐ Are there content elements that need to be added or removed? (If so, make a note and describe them on a separate sheet.)
Feedback	☐ Is the feedback complete and clear? ☐ Does the feedback make learners think? ☐ Does the feedback reflect the consequences of learner actions and decisions before expressing judgments? ☐ Does the feedback provide additional resources for help or exploration? ☐ Does the feedback reinforce a change in behavior? ☐ If feedback is delayed, is it presented at the most effective time?

MANAGING REVIEWS

The value of an iterative process comes from the opportunity to repeatedly review and revise, frequently making course corrections and doing so early enough that the project never departs significantly from the best path. Because the best path for each project may be unique, the critical steps are working up to a point, pausing, reviewing, and making suggestions for improvement before moving on. Whether reviews are completed by each team member individually or together in a meeting, collecting the comments and ideas is a requisite to creating the plan of action for the next iteration.

Effective review requires an understanding of process stages, the purpose of each review, and how to review the associated elements. Reviews require an appreciation for what should be examined and why. They should build on one another in a progression toward the final review.

Every learning product has a variety of many elements (images, activities, projects, interaction formats, dialogue, tests, feedback, and so on) that require repeated review as they move from concept to completion. Below are some of the attributes and questions pertinent to each.

☐ Appropriateness

Does the project meet learner needs as identified in the project plan and the Savvy Start? Are language and media suitable and proper for the audience, culture, and values of the organization?

☐ Correctness

Are media elements accurate and placed properly? Is all text spelled correctly? Is grammar correct?

☐ Functionality

Are instructor notes clear and sufficient? Do all links, navigation, animations, and learner response evaluations work properly? Are performance data captured correctly? Do sessions terminate properly, and are bookmarks functional?

☐ Usability

Are printed materials legible and well organized? Are interactions and controls intuitive and free from ambiguity? Are perceived effort and response time commensurate with the value of each operation? Are all "destructive" events safeguarded from accidental misuse?

☐ Design Consistency

Do all elements adhere to client and team approved design requirements? Are terms, icons, and controls used consistently throughout?

☐ Psychological Impact

Perhaps most often overlooked is how people feel when they participate in a learning experience, but if the experience makes learners uncomfortable, stressed, or unhappy, it's doubtful it will be as successful as it could be. Do users feel victimized? Do they feel burdened and bogged down, or do they feel energized and empowered?

There are also some special considerations to keep in mind concerning appearance, text, functionality, and effectiveness, detailed below.

☐ Appearance

How things look is important. The standard isn't how fancy, modern, or exciting, but rather how effective the visual elements are. Whether it's the color, form, placement, or organization of the visual elements, it is important to review and get this right. The special-purpose prototypes explored various design alternatives and the design proof should set the standard. Subsequent iterations should be reviewed for consistency with the approved design proof.

Some things to check:
- Do colors align to the sponsor's standards?
- Do visuals effectively represent the process or activity?
- Does the interface support the learning and the learner?

☐ Text

Experienced designers know that no matter how important some details may seem at project beginning, text will get a lot of attention in the end. Because most people assume that the iterative process allows many revisions and text is generally very easy to change, all too often little concern is given to text early on. As the product nears completion, long, drawn-out struggles may ensue to get the text perfect.

The words of a course, whether instructional content, feedback, or instructions should not be rewritten repeatedly just for the sake of rewriting. Perhaps because everyone can write, text is the one thing people have the hardest time letting go. It's easy to think that one more review or revision will perfect what is written. Although it may get better, perfection is hard to realize. Good is good.

Early in the process, most of the text will be within sketches, prototypes, and outlines. It's appropriate that it isn't refined. The team should review these materials for completeness of scope rather than specific phrasing or terminology. As the design proof emerges, and then again with production of the alpha release, the team will have the opportunity to review all content as it will be presented to the learner. This is the time for an in-depth review of the words, phrases, terminology, and contextually suitable content.

Some review questions for text include:
- Is it written appropriately for the learner population?
- Is it brief and presented in short segments?
- Is it accurate?
- Does it adequately convey the necessary meaning?
- Are the correct terms used?
- Is it grammatically correct?
- Does it have the right character and personality?
- Does it comply with local, cultural standards?

☐ Functionality

When technology is involved, functionality becomes an especially important concern. You don't want people to think: *I clicked on a button and nothing happened. It says it is loading, but nothing comes up. I am not able to select an item. The feedback doesn't come up when I make a choice. It says I didn't get all the answers correct, but I did!*

If there is an activity that the learner must accomplish and cannot, clearly there is a functional error. Functional errors may even frustrate and limit the reviewer's ability to complete reviews. If the choices cannot be selected, for example, the reviewer cannot see the feedback or the next item.

Just because a course functions as designed, doesn't mean the functionality is acceptable. Functionality is a multifaceted characteristic existing on multiple planes.
- Does it work mechanically?
- Does it have the desired effect as it works?
- Does it contribute to the learning process?
- Is it consistent with learner expectations?
- Is the activity natural and obvious?
- Is it accessible by all individuals who will need access?
- Does it meet with Section 508 accessibility requirements?

☐ Effectiveness

In an iterative process, reviewing for errors comes second to reviewing for effectiveness. There's no need to pull out the errors of something that won't become effective anyway. At every stage in the process, SAM stresses involvement of learners and people other than the designers and developers. It's hard to overstate how surprising it always is that those not grounded in the design and development of a learning product will respond differently than expected.

Reviewing the application for effectiveness is reviewing against the stated performance goals as criteria. Looking for whether a particular learning experience provides an effective instructional opportunity for the learner is much different than scouting for grammatical or other incidental errors. A scenario may be grammatically incorrect while still meeting the measure of effectiveness. On the other hand, lacking careful review, it's possible to have a very well worded piece of learner distraction.

Reviewing for effectiveness does not suggest a full summative review within the development cycle, of course. But then, if not on track to change the

SAM uses iterative formation and summative evaluation.

performance of the learners, a lot of effort and time will have been wasted. In traditional terms, SAM attempts a combination of both formative and summative evaluation within the review cycles, reversing the ADDIE notion that summative evaluations follow formative. We'll get things perfected from a formative viewpoint as soon as we're quite certain we're on a path that will prove effective.

It's easy to be reviewing for instructional effectiveness and get lost in catching little details—missing, as it were, the forest for the trees. Although the design proof may not have much to use for evaluating effectiveness, there is always more to be gained by having it reviewed by prospective learners than anyone ever expects. It's very good practice to sit down with a few learners, fill in the gaps as necessary, and observe their responses.

Some key questions to ensure effectiveness:
- Does each context relate to the learner?
- Does each learning event advance the learner toward performing effective outcome behaviors?
- Does each module give the learner all of the practice necessary to perfect and sustain performance?
- Does each activity present a meaningful, authentic event?
- Is feedback represented in the form of likely consequences?

SETTING EXPECTATIONS FOR ITERATIVE REVIEWS

Early reviews require thinking creatively and broadly to ensure the groundwork is laid for later phases of design and development. Later reviews here in the iterative development phase require more focused reviews, still open-minded of course, to effectively validate progress—or lack thereof.

With the variety of deliverables (prototypes, documents, media, and others) that must be prepared, the team must have aligned expectations for each stage of the process so work can be prepared for the upcoming reviews, check accomplishments, and meet expectations. Before work is done, expectations should be enumerated and agreed to so that there are no surprises and wasted time.

In Table 15-1 are some potential expectations for items feeding the development phase and those produced in it. There will be many criteria for each iteration in the process, but the list provides examples of the changing focus that is important for each review and to keep the process moving.

Table 15-1. Review Expectations for the Development Phase

Deliverable	Review Expectations
Interaction Prototypes	☐ Interactions appropriately address the learning objectives. ☐ The context relates well and realistically to the learner. ☐ The challenge makes sense to the learner. ☐ Activities are authentic and supportive of the challenge. ☐ Learner options are intuitive and easily understood. ☐ Feedback shows consequences of learner activity and decisions.
Project Plan	☐ The plan is complete and realistic. ☐ The plan includes a complete objectives x treatments matrix. ☐ Specific responsibilities are identified by individual or group. ☐ Project expectations are listed. ☐ Project contingencies are identified for when delays and other problems occur.

Media Prototypes	☐ Media elements are appropriate to the age, proficiency, and abilities of the learners. ☐ Media comply with organization's standards, if any. ☐ Media contribute to learning (rather than simply serving as ornamentation). ☐ Redundancy is provided to assist learners with different learning styles and abilities. ☐ Interface for controlling media is intuitive to the presenter or learner.
Content Grid	☐ The grid is complete and provides all content elements needed for each learning event. ☐ Vocabulary (written or spoken) is appropriate for the learners. ☐ Consequences of learner actions can be created and shown within project constraints. ☐ Feedback provides clear guidance and response to the learner's choices. ☐ Adequate resources are available for learners to call upon when needed.
Design Proof	☐ At least one example of every content element is shown at a final level of refinement and in a functional context. ☐ Course flow is fully defined and presented as it will be in the final product. ☐ Navigation, if any, provides learners appropriate and desired options. ☐ All outstanding design or content issues (there should be very few) are clearly identified. ☐ Proof is functionally deliverable via intended mode of instruction, whether classroom, e-learning with LMS, mobile devices, or other.
Alpha	☐ All content is implemented. ☐ Functionality is complete and acceptable with all exceptions documented. ☐ Product can be tested with learners and instructors where appropriate. ☐ All bugs and errors are listed.

Beta	☐ Product is complete and needed corrections identified in testing the alpha release have all been made. ☐ If no problems that must be fixed prior to a release are identified, the beta release becomes the gold release and rolls out for use; otherwise, problems are identified and a second beta release is constructed to repair them.
Gold Release	☐ Product is ready for rollout.

Complete, downloadable checklists for releases can be found online at www.alleni.com/samchecklist.

CONDUCTING A LEARNER REVIEW

When we have learners review instructional products in the process of design and development, they can help validate that we have designed meaningful context, challenge, activity, and feedback; that we have constructed learning experiences that relate to their current needs and understandings; that we have provided authentic opportunities to practice realistic behaviors; that we have composed instructive consequences that provide insight and guidance; that we have matched their ability to comprehend and participate.

Every step of the successive approximation process benefits from the participation of learners. Their reviews affirm the appropriateness of design intentions and assumptions and test development work. This evaluation can come only from those who are required to learn and perform the targeted behaviors. But effectively managing learner reviews is necessary to ensure they have the opportunity to provide relevant and helpful feedback.

Learners are not usually instructional designers and therefore need help providing useful feedback. Depending on the stage of the process (prototype, design proof, alpha, and so on), different types of feedback are helpful. They will need the most guidance when looking at rough prototypes and presumably no guidance when reviewing a beta release. For example, learners may struggle with a review of a prototype without clear directions of what to look for. They need to understand that a prototype is simply a design consideration with perhaps incomplete components. *What would you think if we developed something like this?* Further along in the process, learners will be able to respond to questions, attempt homework assignments, listen to a case study and ask questions, and so on. They can then give their feedback, indicating whether they understood directions, saw the relevance of activities, and felt feedback was clear and helpful.

Many designers are reluctant to involve learners until products are somewhat polished and nearly complete. From my own experience, I must state in the strongest terms that this is a mistake. It's amazing what helpful feedback and insightful suggestions prospective learners can contribute. You would never expect what they can do unless you've tried it.

Another invaluable source of reviews comes from recent learners—people who were, until recently, unable to perform the targeted skills. They are able to remember not knowing how to perform and not being able to. They are able to remember what was most helpful to them in building their new skills. They can identify what was most confusing or most difficult. They can identify what wasn't helpful and what may have wasted time and effort. These are important things to know.

QUALITY ASSURANCE IN SAM

Successive approximation validates the notion that quality is best attained by giving it continuous attention rather than only near the end of product production.

The SAM process has no need for a single, formidable, *"Quality Assurance"* event. In SAM, quality is assessed very often, within each iteration, in fact. And as we have discussed in this chapter, each assessment has specific criteria established ahead of time. Indeed, SAM takes quality so seriously that it is continuously part of the process. There's no need to layer over yet another distinct process.

EVALUATING THE COURSE

Waterfall processes quite logically place evaluation as the last step. With evaluation performed continuously throughout the iterative SAM process, there's much less left to the end. There's much less anxiety about whether the product is deliverable, whether learners will respond positively to it, or whether targeted skills will be developed. There can be a high degree of confidence that the final product will succeed, and yet only success can affirm the achievement.

High scores are easy to obtain at the first two levels of Kirkpatrick's (1959) four-level evaluation model. Having involved learners and iterated designs to get good responses from them, learner reactions (level 1) should be very positive. There should also be little doubt that learning will occur (level 2), as this has been repeatedly verified in the process.

The third and fourth levels are, however, the most important and unfortunately are not so easily verified within the design and development process. Level 3 is achievement of behavioral change. Not only do learners know how to perform more effectively, they actually do it in life, perhaps on the job, where true benefits arise. Level 4 is gathering desired results from changed behaviors. Of course, everyone could have been wrong in the most important assumption of all—that achieving the prescribed behavioral changes would lead to success. In business and in academia, success is defined in many different ways, yet it was presumably the goal that inspired and justified the development of the instructional product. The final, level 4 question is, *Was the goal realized?*

Evaluation external to the SAM process of instructional product design and development is necessary to answer these final questions. Regrettably, and as important as they are, this final feedback which would place the whole of successive approximation in an outer loop of iteration, is too seldom gathered. In those cases where it is, however, SAM seems the perfect process to respond efficiently and effectively to the outcome.

CHAPTER 16

Getting to Gold

Through the iterative process of development, implementation, and evaluation, the last phase of successive approximation takes guidance from the design proof, produces three deliverables: the alpha, beta, and gold releases. As always, each cycle addresses a relatively small amount of work so that evaluation reviews can affirm that the path is correct. If it is not, correction can be made without too much time and effort having been wasted.

THE DELIVERABLES

Alpha Release

Following the design proof, the first deliverable of the development phase is the alpha release. This release is a nearly complete version of the course. The most stringent requirement of the alpha is that missing elements, elements not in final form, and incomplete functionality (bugs), if any, are documented. Reviewers should assume components are as they will be in the released product unless they are called out on an exceptions list.

Prior to the alpha, the team has worked to design the instructional events and define the content scope. The alpha is close to a final product, but in order not to delay reviews longer than necessary, a few components, but only a few, may yet be drafts.

It is sometimes best for multimedia products to delay the incorporation of audio (especially narrative) and video elements until the beta release. Audio can be difficult to change, and video production is more expensive and time consuming to produce. Further, audio and video can be difficult to keep consistent when recorded at other times. Because the alpha review often prompts changes, holding off recordings can save costs. On the other hand, it may be very difficult to evaluate learning experiences without at least scratch media as a stand in. Team experience and media production capabilities will determine the best path.

Beta Release

Following the review of the alpha, the development team will use the suggested revisions to make changes to the product. Additionally, if any development were not completed during the alpha development, it would be completed in production of the beta. These two sets of development activities form the basis of the beta deliverable.

All content and media will be included and in final form. All navigational elements, support information, and additional documentation required by the design will be included as well.

The beta deliverable is an attempt to deliver a completed product. If the team and stakeholders did a thorough job of reviewing the alpha and the team responded diligently, the beta may be deemed the final deliverable product. Indeed, that is the goal. However, if project management has been done well and time and resources remain for additions, there are almost always new ideas, hopes, and wishes that can be fulfilled through another iteration.

Gold

Gold is the goal. Again, the gold version won't be perfect because no product ever is. After release and use, the feedback can be used to iterate at any point in the process. Perhaps just another development cycle is needed. Or perhaps a full but abbreviated pass through all three phases of the SAM process is warranted.

To maintain product life, it can be appropriate to schedule an update iteration of instructional products on a periodic basis. Having all the notes from the previous SAM process can fuel the next run with ideas that had to be set aside previously, but now may be possible.

Production Process

The principles put forth and followed in successive approximation are very similar to those now called Agile software development, Extreme Programming, or SCRUM, but as the developers and supporters of these approaches point out, they are useful for managing many types of projects, not just software development projects. It's reassuring to see that software development groups have picked up the same notions that successive approximation users have long been advocating for instructional product development. For example, "Extreme Programming empowers your developers to confidently respond to changing customer requirements, even late in the life cycle" (www.extremeprogramming.org, accessed 1/18/12).

The Agile Manifesto lists the following points of value that hold great appeal for the development of instructional products as well.

Table 16-1. Values Listed by the Agile Manifesto

TRADITIONAL VALUES	VALUED MORE
Processes and tools	Individuals and interactions
Comprehensive documentation	Working software
Contract negotiation	Customer collaboration
Following a plan	Responding to change

On the next page the Agile Manifesto (reproduced with permission) is directly applicable to the development of instructional products. Substitute "courseware" or "instructional materials" for "software."

Agile Manifesto

Our highest priority is to satisfy the customer through early and continuous delivery of valuable software.

Welcome changing requirements, even late in development. Agile processes harness change for the customer's competitive advantage.

Deliver working software frequently, from a couple of weeks to a couple of months, with a preference to the shorter timescale.

Business people and developers must work together daily throughout the project.

Build projects around motivated individuals. Give them the environment and support they need, and trust them to get the job done.

The most efficient and effective method of conveying information to and within a development team is face-to-face conversation.

Working software is the primary measure of progress.

Agile processes promote sustainable development. The sponsors, developers, and users should be able to maintain a constant pace indefinitely.

Continuous attention to technical excellence and good design enhances agility.

Simplicity—the art of maximizing the amount of work not done—is essential.

The best architectures, requirements, and designs emerge from self-organizing teams.

At regular intervals, the team reflects on how to become more effective, then tunes and adjusts its behavior accordingly.

Source: www.agilemanifesto.org.

The chart in Figure 16-1 visualizes the completion of product development by deliverable. The largest development advancement occurs between the design proof and the alpha deliverable. The alpha is the first deliverable following design approval as defined by the design proof and incorporates all content, whereas the design proof contains only examples of content. The following beta and gold releases provide only refinements, diminishing in volume and significance.

Figure 16-1. Levels of Product Completion in the Savvy Process

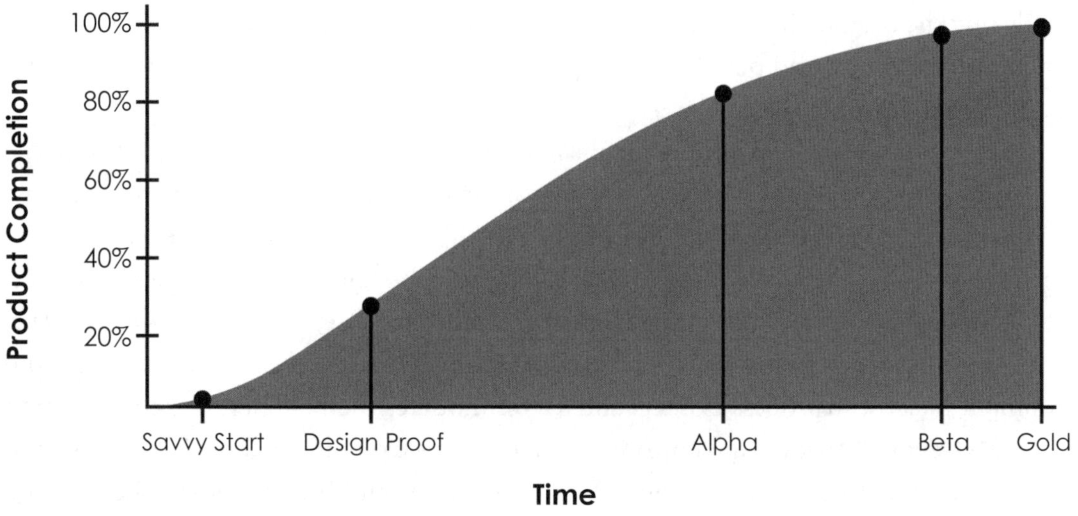

Because so many content components are involved in large projects, it may be helpful to segment content and plan extra iterations to address one segment at a time.

The power of iterative methods is that they provide a clear pathway from collaborative brainstorming, through iterative design efforts, to clear development targets for review and revision. And yet, they allow—actually expect—changes to be requested at any point. Even after a product rolls out, in terms of the process, this is just considered a point of evaluation. No product ever reaches perfection, so it's far better to get a functional product in use and take advantage of observed results than continue infinite revisions and never release anything.

Key risks are missed expectations and expanding scope. While these deterrents to success are present throughout the process, they can become particularly meddlesome in the final phases.

Missed Expectations

Every team member and stakeholder develops and comes to hold certain expectations for what the outcome will be—what the product will look and feel like, what the learning experiences will be, what performance will result. Although some may suspend strongly held expectations through the design phase, concerns can become more concrete and uncontainable as the product becomes tangible. They finally burst forth as urgent issues: *I hate to say this now, but I'm really worried.*

The reason for expressing expectations so late in the process is two-fold: 1) people may have hoped the design process would gravitate to their idea of good instruction (*I'm sure they'll find a good way of dealing with this*), or 2) people didn't gain a clear picture of the design during the design phase. Sometimes expectations aren't easy to share until a product becomes fairly complete and people realize, perhaps for the first time, that it isn't becoming what they hoped it would become.

In many cases, however, it's simply (as discussed in chapter 14) that good ideas emerge whenever they wish, and they have a tendency to arrive late. This is why giving serious attention to the design proof is so very important. It's the first point in the cycle where enough of the components have come together that the feeling of the final product is evident.

But SAM and all the iterative processes are, if nothing else, realistic processes. And because it's common, perhaps unavoidable, that changes will be desired even within the development phase, the process expects and accommodates them. When working in small chunks with frequent reviews and constant contact with stakeholders, most ideas requiring changes can be identified in the earliest iterations. Fewer and fewer major issues will be found as the product nears completion.

Expanding Scope

The dreaded *scope change, scope creep,* or *out-of-scope* additions are aspersions intended to incriminate requested changes that cannot be accomplished without added resources, missed deadlines, more money, or more effort. As with missed expectations, SAM pushes hard to get agreement as early as possible, but then also provides resources for handling late changes because they are inevitable.

While the iterative design phase reduces the risk of pursuing a poor design by communicating a variety of design options and alternatives, scope limitations are most apparent when the product finally comes together in later deliverables. Smartly, even the final development iterations accommodate some changes—whether enough is always something of skill and art developed by experienced project managers.

LET THE GOOD TIMES ROLL

With any undertaking as complex as developing instructional products, there are always hurdles to overcome. An SME is not available, a reviewer is on vacation, a writer or developer is working on another project. Each one poses barriers to a timely delivery of a quality product. One strategy to overcome these barriers is "rolling" the deliverable.

Rolling simply refers to continuing to progress on the areas that can move ahead while waiting for the resources to be available for the others. For example, when building a three-module course and planning to deliver the alpha on schedule, the writer still has work to complete on another project and can only dedicate 20 hours per week to this one. The choices are 1) push the alpha deliverable by a couple of weeks to give the writer time to complete the work, or 2) deliver two alphas—one containing the first module and the second containing the other two. Rolling the deliverable in this way keeps the project moving and gives the review team their work on schedule.

DEBRIEF

Following acceptance of the gold deliverable, teams often find it useful to reassemble to discuss their thoughts about the project, the product, and the process. Is there anything they would do differently next time? Taking some time to review and make notes can lay a solid foundation for the next project (see Tables 16-2 and 16-3 on the next pages). Indeed, iteration is not only a great way to produce superlative products, it's also a primary means of improving the process itself.

Table 16-2. Alpha Review Checklist for e-Learning Projects

Navigation	☐ Recheck all design proof navigation items. ☐ Were navigational elements modified, added, or removed as requested? ☐ Do new or modified elements function fully as designed? ☐ Do all windows (pop-ups) have close/continue buttons? ☐ If there are learner-accessible course resources, are all of them now loaded, available, and displaying appropriately? ☐ Is the course exit or completion handled appropriately?
Media	☐ Recheck all design proof media items. ☐ Were media elements modified, added, or removed as requested? ☐ Are all media loading correctly and appearing in a timely manner? ☐ Are all media appealing, of appropriate quality, and suitable for the audience? ☐ Is all needed graphical or video content integrated into the application and displaying properly? ☐ Are graphics clear, readable, and understandable? ☐ Are all sounds properly synchronized? ☐ Is text free of errors? (Check for typos, spelling and grammatical errors, truncation, color, font, etc.) ☐ Is all text written at an acceptable reading level? ☐ Are there any places where media should be revised to improve impact?
Interaction	☐ Recheck all design proof interaction items. ☐ Were interaction elements modified, added, or removed as requested? ☐ Are all designed interactions now present and sequenced properly? ☐ Do all interactions process learner responses correctly, including unusual or unexpected responses? ☐ If the learner re-encounters an interaction, does it behave as desired? ☐ Are learner responses recorded properly, per design? ☐ Are scores computed properly, even if scored activities are interrupted and continued or restarted?

Content	☐ Recheck all design proof content items. ☐ Were content elements modified, added, or removed as requested? ☐ Are all of the instructional objectives addressed effectively by the interactions and content? ☐ Is the content organized logically and effectively from the learner's viewpoint? ☐ Are learners given adequate opportunities to evaluate their progress? ☐ Is sufficient practice provided?
Feedback	☐ Recheck all design proof feedback items. ☐ Were feedback elements modified, added, or removed as requested? ☐ Is all feedback clear and meaningful to the learner? ☐ Do all feedback boxes/windows provide clear navigation? ☐ Is there any section or interaction that is missing feedback?

Table 16-3. Beta Review Checklist for e-Learning Projects

Navigation	☐ Recheck all alpha navigation items. ☐ Were navigational elements modified, added, or removed as requested?
Media	☐ Recheck all alpha media items. ☐ Were media elements modified, added, or removed as requested?
Interaction	☐ Recheck all alpha interaction items. ☐ Were interaction elements modified, added, or removed as requested?
Content	☐ Recheck all alpha content items. ☐ Were content elements modified, added, or removed as requested?
Feedback	☐ Recheck all alpha feedback items. ☐ Were feedback elements modified, added, or removed as requested?

References

Allen, M. (2002). *Michael Allen's Guide to e-Learning.* New Jersey: Wiley.

Allen, M. (2006). *Creating Successful e-Learning: A Rapid System for Getting It Right First Time, Every Time.* San Francisco: Pfeiffer.

Allen, M. (2007). *Designing Successful e-Learning: Forget What You Know About Instructional Design and Do Something Interesting.* San Francisco: Pfeiffer.

Allen, M. (2011). *Successful e-Learning Interface: Making Learning Technology Polite, Effective, and Fun.* San Francisco: Pfeiffer.

Allen, M. and Lipshutz, M. (In Press). *Managing e-Learning Development: Creating Dramatic Successes Even With Outrageous Timelines, Budgets, and Expectations.* San Francisco: Pfeiffer.

Bichelmeyer, B.A. (2005). "The ADDIE Model: A Metaphor for the Lack of Clarity in the Field of IDT," http://www.indiana.edu/~idt/shortpapers/documents/IDTf_Bic.pdf (accessed November 18, 2009).

Buxton, B. (2007). *Sketching User Experiences: Getting the Design Right and the Right Design.* San Francisco: Morgan Kaufmann Publishers.

Carliner, S. and M. Driscoll. (2009). Who's Creating the E-Learning. In *Michael Allen's 2009 e-Learning Annual,* ed. Michael Allen (Vol. 1, 43-56). San Francisco: Pfeiffer.

Gustafson, K.L. and R.M. Branch. (2002). What Is Instructional Design? In *Trends and Issues in Instructional Design and Technology,* eds. R.A. Resier and J.V. Dempsey. Columbus: OH, Merrill Prentice Hall.

Kirkpatrick, D.L. (1959). *Evaluating Training Programs, 2nd ed.* San Francisco: Berrett-Koehler.

Kruse, K. (2009). "Introduction to Instructional Design and the ADDIE Model," http://www.transformativedesigns.com/id_systems.html.

Mager, R. (1997). *Preparing Instructional Objectives: A Critical Tool in the Development of Effective Instruction.* Atlanta: Center for Effective Performance, Inc.

Molenda, M. (2003). In Search of the Elusive ADDIE Model. *Performance Improvement, 42*(5), 34-36.

Molenda, M., C.M. Reigeluth, and L.M. Nelson. (2003). Instructional Design. In *Encyclopedia of Cognitive Science* (Vol. 2, pp. 574–578), ed. L. Nadel. London: Nature Publishing Group.

Piskurich, George M. (2000). *Rapid Instructional Design: Learning ID Fast and Right.* San Francisco: Jossey-Bass.

Rossett, A. (1999). *First Things Fast: A Handbook for Performance Analysis.* San Francisco: Jossey-Bass.

Visscher-Voerman, I. and K.L. Gustafson. (2004). *Paradigms in the Theory and Practice of Education and Training Design.* Educational Technology, Research and Development, 52(2).

Yanchar, S.C., J.B. South, D.D. Williams, and B.G. Wilson. (2007). How Do Instructional Designers Use Theory? A Qualitative-Developmental Study of the Integration of Theory and Technology. In *Proceedings of the Association for Educational Communication and Technology* (Vol.1, pp. 332-337), ed. M. Simonson. Anaheim, CA: AECT.Allen, M. (2002). *Michael Allen's Guide to e-Learning.* New Jersey: Wiley.

Other Selected Works by Michael Allen

Michael Allen's Guide to e-Learning (Wiley, 2002)

Michael Allen's e-Learning Library Series

> Book 1: *Creating Successful e-Learning: A Rapid System for Getting It Right First Time, Every Time* (Pfeiffer, 2006)

> Book 2: *Designing Successful e-Learning: Forget What You Know About Instructional Design and Do Something Interesting* (Pfeiffer, 2007)

> Book 3: *Successful e-Learning Interface: Making Learning Technology Polite, Effective, and Fun* (Pfeiffer, 2011)

Michael Allen's e-Learning Annual Series

> *Michael Allen's 2008 e-Learning Annual* (Pfeiffer, 2008)

> *Michael Allen's 2009 e-Learning Annual* (Pfeiffer, 2009)

> *Michael Allen's 2012 e-Learning Annual* (Pfeiffer, 2011)

About the Authors

Michael Allen

Michael Allen, PhD, is a recognized leader in e-learning. He has made career-long contributions by inventing and sharing effective interactive multimedia learning strategies and authoring tools. He has nearly 45 years of professional, academic, and corporate experience in teaching, developing, and marketing interactive learning and performance support systems; and he has led teams of doctorate-level specialists in learning research, instructional design, computer-based training, and human engineering. For decades, he has concentrated on defining unique methods of  instructional design and development that provide meaningful and memorable learning experiences through "true" cognitive interactivity. He shares his insights through his writing, speaking, seminars, and examples. He is now, once again, developing software to ease the development of excellent learning experiences and help children creatively express "what they know."

In May 2011, he received ASTD's Distinguished Contribution to Workplace Learning and Performance Award. In May 2012, Allen was selected by The National Ethnic Coalition of Organizations (NECO) Advisory Committee as a recipient of the 2012 Ellis Island Medal of Honor.

Allen is currently chairman & CEO of Allen Interactions Inc. His clients include the most known and respected public corporations and professional associations.

Allen was the director of advanced educational systems research and development of Control Data Corporation's famous PLATO computer-based education system used around the world. He was the founder, and former chairman of Authorware, Inc. and also the primary architect of *Authorware Professional*, which was based on Allen's extensive research on creativity and creative problem-solving. It became a groundbreaking authoring tool combining power and ease of use, and ultimately the industry standard. Authorware, Inc. merged with Macromind/Paracomp to become Macromedia, which was later acquired by Adobe.

Allen is once again determined to conquer the perplexing idiosyncrasies and complexities of interactive media so that all people can share their knowledge, experience, and insights through it. Just now coming on the market is ZebraZapps—a revolutionary cloud-based authoring and publishing platform that allows anyone to create and deploy compelling interactive multimedia in a way that nothing else can. In fact, experiments have shown that 10-year-olds can create media-rich interactive applications as homework that demonstrate what they know. Even high-end programmers cannot program such applications in the time children can build them with Zebra.

His first book, *Michael Allen's Guide to e-Learning: Building Interactive, Fun, and Effective Learning Programs for Any Company,* has been praised by industry experts as the e-learning textbook that everyone, from beginners to experts, must have. It is the primary text for ASTD's e-learning design certificate programs and countless other programs worldwide. The *Guide* served as the jumping off point for *Michael Allen's e-Learning Series,* a six-volume series covering a range of topics with three books currently complete. Michael Allen also serves as editor of *Michael Allen's e-Learning Annuals* series, which has been noted as a "phenomenal resource" for scholars and practitioners alike, carrying up-to-date controversies from renowned experts.

Allen holds MA and PhD degrees in educational psychology from The Ohio State University. He is an adjunct professor at the University of Minnesota School of Medicine and is working in association with the university and the National Institutes of Health to develop interactive interventions to reduce the spread of HIV and AIDS.

Richard Sites

Richard H. Sites, EdD, has spent the past 15 years designing and implementing web-based training and tools to support improved workplace performance. His efforts have been in both academia and private industry, including working with many Fortune 500 companies. He is Vice President of Client Services for Allen Interactions Inc., where he is responsible

for promoting value-driven consulting and design throughout all Allen Interactions partnerships.

Before joining Allen Interactions, Richard held a faculty position and served as the director of the Educator Performance Institute at the University of West Florida. Richard was the lead designer of a nationally marketed web-based training system to support educators with the design of standards-based instruction. In addition to his e-learning experience, Richard's 15 years of instructional experience have been focused on high quality e-learning, including the design and development of various nationally recognized educator training products, teaching graduate courses in instructional design and media, and speeches at national and regional educational conferences.

Richard earned a doctorate of education in curriculum and instruction, specializing in instructional technology, from the University of West Florida. His doctoral research focused on the design of a model for scaffolding in a web-based performance support system. Richard also earned a master's of education and a bachelor's of business administration.

About Allen Interactions

Allen Interactions has pioneered the e-learning industry since the first authoring tools were developed in 1985. The company was founded by CEO, Michael Allen, and associates in 1993 to assist multimedia professionals in building engaging interactive learning solutions. On the leading edge for two decades, they have invented and reinvented the most powerful learning paradigms, cost-effective tools, and successful creative processes in the industry.

Allen Interactions specialties include e-learning, blended learning, and a wide variety of technology-enabled solutions customized for specific performance improvement. Other services include consulting and training services, and tool and software development. Their award-winning custom design and development services have been commissioned by Apple, American Express, Bank of America, Boston Scientific, Comcast, Delta Air Lines, Disney, Ecolab, Essilor, Hilton, HSBC, IBM, Medtronic, Merck, Microsoft, Motorola, Nextel, UPS, Travelocity, and hundreds of other leading corporations.

Allen Interactions is home to the revolutionary new authoring system called ZebraZapps. Another remarkable vision of Allen, ZebraZapps is a cloud-based authoring system that gives anyone, from experienced developers to children, the ability to create rich interactive media applications, quickly and easily. Applications created with ZebraZapps can be shared, published, and even sold in the online shops. From concept to creation, ZebraZapps provides a fun, fast, what-you-see-is-what-you-get (WYSIWYG) interface.

Allen Interactions has offices across the country, with corporate headquarters in Minnesota. They can be reached at alleninteractions.com or by phone at (800) 799-6280.

Index

A

Active learning, 116
Activity, of learning events, 26–27
Adaptation, 17–18
ADDIE model
    criticism of, 13
    cyclical, 17
    definition of, 13
    early version of, 14–15
    evaluations, 175
    feedback in, 107–108
    foundational notions of, 13, 15
    high level view of, 13
    iterative, 17
    limitations of, 19
    manageable nature of, 32
    modification of, 17–18
Additional design, 43–45, 157–158
Agenda
    rapid prototyping, 105
    Savvy Start, 65–69, 72
Agile Manifesto, 183–184
Alpha release, 47, 177, 181–182, 185, 188–189
Analysis paralysis, 6
Appearance, of project, 176
Appropriateness, of project, 175
Approvals, 132
Assessments, 117–119, 124
Authentic activity, 26–27

B

Backgrounding/background information, 40–41,
        58–60, 76, 107, 124
Behavioral change, 51–52, 117
Behavioral objectives, 111
Best ideas, 162, 186
Beta 2, 48
Beta release, 47, 178, 182, 185, 189
Brainstorming
    collaborative nature of, 102, 185
    description of, 41, 44, 109
    group, 102
    ideas from, 90, 92
    Savvy Start team participation in, 64
    tips on, 102–103
Breadth, 121–122
Budget, 130

C

CCAF, 27–28
Challenges
    instructional programs, 3
    in learning events, 25–26
    learning through, 25
Clients
    informing of, 49
    setting expectations for, 50
Collaboration, 31
Compliancy issues, 124
Conditions of performance, 24
Consequences, 27
Consultant, 49
Content
    information gathering for, 165
    multimedia, 131
    pre-existing, 115–116
    prototyping and, 103
    writing of, 164–168
Content development plan, 43
Content grids, 164–168, 177
Content style guide, 43
Context, of learning event, 24–25
Continuous evaluation, 16, 179
Course content, 164–168
Course evaluation, 179–180
Credibility, 13

D

Debriefing, 187–189
Decision making, 132
Delegation, 132
Deliverables
    alpha release, 47, 177, 181–182, 185, 188–189
    beta release, 47, 178, 182, 185, 189
    gold release, 48, 178, 182, 185
    rolling the, 187
Delivery platform, 130–131
Design consistency, of project, 176
Design documentation, 6
Design models, 4
Design proof
    changes during, 164
    components of, 163
    description of, 46, 97, 162–163
    redesign after, 164
    review of, 169–171, 177
    time spent on, 163–164

Disrespect, 5
Distributed practice, 22
Documentation, 6, 132–133

E
Effectiveness
    of iterative process, 175
    of process model, 31–32
Efficiency, of process model, 31–32
E-learning
    advantages of, 118
    assessment benefits of, 118
    beta review checklist for, 189
    challenging of learners through, 25
    delivery platform, 130
    description of, 21–22
    design proof, reviewing of, 170–171
    development time in, 163
    interactivity in, 25, 84, 101
    learner abilities and readiness assessments, 118
    LMS interface compliancy issues, 124
    prototype, 92, 94–97
    tools for development of, 101
    visual interactivity in, 101
E-sketches, 87–89
Evaluation
    continuous, 16, 179
    four-level model of, 179–180
    frequency of, 123
    iterative, 169–180
Expectations
    client, 50
    cost, 130
    expressing of, 186
    iterative reviews, 176–178
    missed, 186
    support team creation based on, 65
Extreme Programming, 183

F
"Facts," 6–7
Familiarity, 13
Feedback, 27, 107–108, 178
Formative evaluation, 175
Functional errors, 177
Functional prototypes, 44–45, 84
Functionality, of project, 175, 177

G
Goals
    design focus on, 75
    learning, 74–75
    performance, 77–78
    setting of, 109–110

Gold release, 48, 178, 182, 185
Group brainstorming, 102

H
Hardware, 131
Human resources staff, 64

I
Ideal process model
    collaboration, 31
    effectiveness, 31–32
    efficiency, 31–32
    iterative process, 30–31
    manageable nature of, 32–33
    overview of, 29–30
Ideas, 162, 186
Imitation, 24
Individualization, 118–119
Information, 9
Information gathering
    background information, 40–41, 58–60, 76, 107
    in course content development, 165
Instructional design
    definition of, 11–12
    outcome of, 12
    as profession, 8
    requirements needed for, 8
    SAM leader's skills in, 52
Instructional designer, 51, 63
Instructional events
    building of, 104–105
    learning goals and objectives achieved with, 51
Instructional objectives, 110–114, 119
Instructional programs, 3
Instructional systems design
    complexity associated with, 16
    steps involved in, 12
Instructional systems development models
    adaptation of, 17–18
    description of, 1
Integrated prototypes, 44
Interactive learning events, 23–28
Intuition, 30
ISD models. *See* Instructional systems development models
Iterative design phase
    additional design, 43–45, 157–158
    description of, 42–45
    project planning. *See* Project planning
    prototyping in, 106. *See also* Prototype(s); Prototyping
    purpose of, 80
    Savvy Start and, differences between, 80
    schematic diagram of, 40, 42, 74, 123, 127, 133, 159

Iterative development phase
  alpha release from, 47, 177, 181–182, 185, 188–189
  beta release from, 47, 178, 182, 185, 188
  description of, 45–48
  design proof. *See* Design proof
  gold release from, 48, 178, 182, 185
  production process, 183–185
  review expectations for, 176–178
  schematic diagram of, 40, 45, 74, 123, 133, 159
Iterative processes
  approximations created by, 161
  basic, 30–31
  best ideas and, 162, 186
  description of, 128, 157
  design proof produced by. *See* Design proof
  effectiveness reviews, 175
  power of, 185
  realistic nature of, 186
  in SAM1, 33–36, 42
  in SAM2, 42–48
  Savvy Start. *See* Savvy Start
Iterative reviews
  management of, 172–175
  setting expectations for, 176–178

J
Judgments, 27

L
Leader. *See* SAM leader
Learner-centered approach, 52
Learners
  abilities and readiness assessments, 118
  attention of, 4
  boring instruction effects on, 4–5
  challenging of, 25–26
  disrespect of, 5
  experimentation with involvement, 14
  interests of, 7
  learning program design involvement by, 8
  meaningful learning events effect on, 22
  motivated, 23
  needs and wants of, 7
  negative attitudes of, 4
  recent, 179
  review of instructional products by, 178–179
  SAM leader as advocate of, 52
  on Savvy Start team, 63
  self-image of, 4
  user testing with, 123
  validation with, 123
Learning
  e-. *See* E-learning
  from mistakes, 30

  through imitation, 24
  through observation, 23–24
Learning events
  activities included in, 26–27
  assessments needed for, 117–119
  challenges included in, 25–26
  characteristics of, 22–23
  components of, 23–28
  context of, 24–25
  defining of, 21
  feedback included in, 27
  interactive, 23–28
  meaningful, 22, 28
  measurable, 23, 28
  memorable, 22–23, 28
  motivational, 23, 28
  specifying of, 15
Learning experiences, 6, 77, 119
Learning goals, 74–75
Learning programs
  analysis paralysis, 6
  "facts," 6–7
  poor, reasons for, 5–9
  risk management uses of, 5–6
Linear process, 16, 31
LMS, 124, 158
Look-and-feel prototype, 158

M
Macro assessment, 117
Manageable process, 32–33
Management, 3
Meaningful learning events, 22, 25, 28
Meaningfulness, 25
Measurable learning events, 23, 28
Media, 124–125
Media artist, 51–52
Media prototypes, 44, 158, 177
Media style guide, 43
Memorable learning events, 22–23, 28
Micro assessment, 117–119
Mistakes
  learning from, 30
  in prototyping, 103
Motivational learning events, 23, 28
Multimedia content, 131
Multimedia products, 182
Multiple-choice questions, 26

N
Navigation prototype, 158
Negative attitudes, 4
Negotiation skills, 51
Network prototype, 158

O

Objectives, instructional, 110–114, 119
Objectives x treatments matrix, 111–115, 119, 161
Observation, 23–24
Opinions, 9
Organization
  media selection affected by culture of, 125
  training environment of, 75–76

P

Performance goals, 77–78
Performance tracking, 124
PERT chart, 32
Phases
  approval of, 5
  iterative design. *See* Iterative design phase
  iterative development. *See* Iterative development phase
  preparation. *See* Preparation phase
Post-tests, 117
PowerPoint, 101
Pre-existing content, 115–116
Preparation phase
  backgrounding, 40–41, 58–60, 76, 107
  definition of, 40
  overview of, 57, 123
  Savvy Start. *See* Savvy Start
  schematic diagram of, 40, 57, 74, 133, 159
  speed of, 41, 57
Priorities, 129
Problem behaviors, 78
Process
  iterative. *See* Iterative processes
  organizational issues that affect, 60
  selection of, 14
Process model, ideal. *See* Ideal process model
Production process, 183–185
Project costs, 130
Project leader. *See* SAM leader
Project manager
  description of, 49
  priority setting by, 129
  role of, 51
  on Savvy Start team, 63
Project plan, 134–156, 176
Project planning
  approvals, 132
  costs, 130
  decision making, 132
  delivery platform, 130–131
  description of, 43, 127–128
  documentation, 132–133
  focus of, 128
  initial, 128–131

priorities, 129
responsibilities, 132
sample plan, 134–156
subject matter experts, 131–132
Project review, 172–175
Project sponsor, 59–60
Project team, 64–65, 132
Prototype(s)
  benefits of, 90–92
  building of, 104–105
  characteristics of, 92–93
  content development for, 116, 164–168
  definition of, 92
  description of, 34, 36, 42
  disposable nature of, 98, 121
  early access to, 108
  e-learning, 92, 94–97
  evaluation of, 106–107
  feedback about, 107–108
  first version of, 96, 98
  functional, 44–45, 84
  instructional events, 104–105
  Integrated, 44
  interim, 92
  lifecycle of, 94–97
  media, 44, 158, 177
  purpose of, 83, 90
  reasons for building, 84–92
  reviewing of, 105–108, 169, 176
  rules for working with, 98
  second version of, 96, 98
  sketches and, 83–84, 86–87
  special-purpose, 44, 93, 157–158, 173
  speed as measure of success with, 93
  summary of, 108
  third version of, 97–98
  types of, 44–45
  user feedback about, 107–108
  versions of, 96–97
  walkthrough of, 106
Prototyper
  advice for, 102
  on Savvy Start team, 63
  selection of, 99–100
  traits of, 99
Prototyping
  content considerations, 103
  importance of, 81
  mistakes made in, 103
  rapid, 93, 104–105
  in Savvy Start, 106
  tips on, 102–103
  tools for, 100–103
  unanticipated discoveries during, 107

Psychological impact, of project, 176

Q

Quality assurance, 179

R

Rapid prototyping, 93, 104–105
Remote learning, 130
Reviews. *See also* Iterative reviews
    design proof, 169–171
    learner, 178–179
    project, 172–175
    prototypes, 105–108, 169, 176
Risk management, 5–6
Role-playing, 158
Rolling, 187
Rollout, 48

S

SAM
    advantages of, 55, 108
    description of, 1, 33, 73
    disadvantages of, 122
    focus of, 121
    goal-oriented design versus, 75
    integrated design and development in, 33
    learner involvement, 175, 178–179
    learning created using, 50
    level 1. *See* SAM1
    liability of, 122
    overview of, 74
    principles of, 73
    prototyping. *See* Prototyping
    quality assurance in, 179
    rapid collaborative design as foundation of, 128
    realistic nature of, 186
    Savvy Start team's understanding of, 73–74
    start dates for, 133
SAM1
    advantages of, 38
    challenges for, 37–38
    evaluation of, 36–37
    integrated design and development in, 61
    iterative processes in, 33–36, 42
    overview of, 33–36
    perpetual cycling associated with, 37–38
    refining of work and, 37
    SAM2 versus, 42
    simplicity of, 38
SAM2
    additional design, 43–45, 157–158
    alpha release, 47, 177, 181–182, 185, 188–189
    background information, 40–41, 58–60, 76
    beta release, 47, 178, 182, 185, 189
    design proof, 46
    gold release, 48, 178, 182, 185

    iterative design phase of, 42–45
    iterative development phase of, 45–48
    overview of, 39–40
    preparation phase of. *See* Preparation phase
    project planning, 43
    projects using, 162–163
    prototypes, 42, 44–45
    SAM1 versus, 42
    Savvy Start. *See* Savvy Start
    schematic diagram of, 40, 42, 74
SAM leader
    behavior change as focus of, 51–52
    consulting skills of, 53
    design and project variables adjusted by, 51
    expectations setting and maintenance by, 50
    leadership skills of, 50
    as learner advocate, 52
    negotiation skills of, 51
    preparedness checklist for, 52–54
    project management skills of, 53
    responsibilities of, 50
    roles of, 51
    self-assessments, 52–54
    selling skills of, 53
Savvy Start
    activities completed before starting, 74
    activities included in, 65
    agenda of, 65–69, 72
    benefits of, 61, 81
    collaborative atmosphere of, 71
    conducting of, 70–79
    criteria for success, 77
    customizing of, 69–70
    definition of, 41, 60
    elements of, 61
    focus of, 71, 74
    ground rules of, 72–73
    highlights of, 42
    information obtained from, 128
    iterative design phase and, differences between, 80
    kick-off, 66, 71–72
    learning goals stated in, 74–75
    performance goals, 77–78
    planning of, 62
    previous work reviewed during, 76
    prototyping in, 106
    purpose of, 60–61, 80
    questions answered during, 80–81
    refreshing the content of, 122
    room preparation for, 70
    second, 80–81
    skills hierarchy, 78–79
    time requirements, 43
    training environment of organization examined
        during, 75–76

Savvy Start summary report, 43
Savvy Start team
    brainstorming participation by, 64
    building of, 62–65
    goal-oriented design as focus of, 75
    human resources staff involvement in, 64
    learners on, 63
    legal staff involvement in, 64
    members of, 63
    project team created from, 64–65
    SAM understanding by, 73–74
    storytelling by, 76–77
    subject matter experts on, 62
    support team created from, 64–65
Scope, 186
SCRUM, 183
Self-image, 4
Setting of expectations, 50, 176–178. *See also*
        Expectations
Shareholders, 3
Sketches
    e-, 87–89
    examples of, 84, 88–89
    prototypes and, 84, 86–87
Sketching, 83–84, 94–95
Skills hierarchy, 78–79
Software versioning, 131
Solutions, 123–124
Special-purpose prototypes, 44, 93, 157–158, 173

Specification documents, 37
Sponsor, 59–60
Stakeholders, 64
Storytelling, 76–77
Subject aversion, 4
Subject matter experts, 62, 131–132
Success
    criteria for, 77
    designing for, 121–125
Successive approximation model. *See* SAM
Summative evaluation, 175
Supervisor training, 60
Support team, 64–65

T
"Teaching the test," 117
"Tell-and-test" instruction, 6
Text, of project, 176–177
Traditional design models, 3, 5
Training departments, 3, 5
Training designers, 7

U
Usability, of project, 175
User testing, 123

W
Waterfall concept/process, 16, 31, 179
Working backward, 114–115